CONTE[

MW00878040

1

Personal names have been changed.

All Bible verses are quoted from the New King James Version unless otherwise noted.

ASV--American Standard Version
KJV--King James Version
NAS--New American Standard
NLT--New Living Testament
THE MESSAGE—contemporary language

ACKNOWLEDGMENTS

There are many awesome teachers in my life during the ~~twenty-nine~~ years I have walked with the Lord. The first person I want to recognize is my mother, who now walks on the golden streets of heaven and never stopped praying for me or believing that Yahweh (Creator God of the universe) would one day bring me back to His Kingdom.

41

Another person who prayed me into the Kingdom is my long-time friend, Nancy Davies.

My foster mom took me from a wayward, hating, hurting creature to the person I am today. I will forever be indebted to my wonderful Nina, who took in a very troubled teenager and encouraged her to become all she could be. By experiencing God's unconditional love through the kindest, most gentle and caring individual I've ever met, I learned to have the confidence and strength to do anything and everything I wanted.

I also acknowledge George Kilby, who taught the Bible studies at the community church (see "Charlatans"). I soaked in the Living Water he poured out. He is spirit-filled and leads a holy, dedicated life to God. I don't even know if he is still sojourning on this earth as he was in his late fifties when I knew him.

Next are Pastors Norma and Bruce Montroy, who definitely changed my diapers and gave me bottles those first few years of my babyhood as a Christian. I am fed continually by their daily devotional on spearministries.org and regularly consult them on spiritual issues.

My Spiritual mom, June Henry, has always been there when I need a friend, confidant, or prayer warrior. She is a mighty intercessor who is filled with wisdom, and I count it a privilege to know her!

I am indebted to Aglow International because its vision is global and produces sound teachings on the power of the Holy Spirit. It is a pioneer of God's purposes in the earth. At one of its conventions, I first learned about replacement theology (the church has replaced the Jews as God's chosen) and how detrimental that line of thinking is to the body of Christ. For God's promises to the Jews are unchangeable and irrevocable: "I will bless those that bless thee and curse those that curse thee!" I attribute much of my spiritual growth to being involved with this ministry. Jane Hansen-Hoyt (the international president) is a role model to women around the world.

I would also be remiss if I didn't mention Special Touch Ministries to physically and mentally challenged people. It provides a wonderful camp in various parts of the country, monthly and quarterly chapter meetings, and a very informative newsletter. God has taught me to appreciate the things I used to take for granted—like walking, talking, and breathing! When I come back from camp, I *have no problems*!

I thank our wonderful little church in Fillmore, Utah, for helping me financially to publish this book!

Two ladies did the final proof and I appreciate their fine tuning so much! Thank you Mary Jane Peterson and another faithful friend who wants to remain anonymous.

Last, but definitely not *least*, is my wonderful husband, Jon, who loves me, admires me, and encourages me daily. I bask in the sunshine of his love.

Now walking the streets of gold.)
haveing fought the "good" fight!

ABIDING IN THE VINE

John 15:1–2 – I am the true vine, and My Father is the vine dresser. Every branch in Me that does not bear fruit, He takes away; and every branch that bears fruit, He prunes it so that it may bear more fruit. NAS

Many years ago, when I had been a Christian for about five years, I was at Living Waters Retreat Center. Sitting on the bank of Oak Creek, I was looking at this spindly twig growing out of the ground. Then I saw this massive tree across the stream with huge limbs and a myriad of big green leaves. I lamented, "Ooohh, I want to be like that giant tree over there; offering shade and rest to all. I want to grow an abundance of fruits. I'm so tired of being like that skinny tree!"

Then came the Still, Small Voice singing to an old 70s rock 'n roll tune: "Slow down, you move too fast. You gotta make our times together last. Don't you know you're the apple of my eye? Don't you know my love for you will never die?"

I have since counseled many young Christians with advice I know comes from the Holy Spirit. We do not expect a two-year old to perform like a thirty-year old. Thus, we should not be so hard on ourselves when we cannot accomplish the feats of a veteran Christian. Yahweh has our best interests in mind, and He will complete the work He started in us. (Philippians 1:6: "Being confident of this very thing that He who began a good work in you will perform it until the day of Jesus Christ.") We have to be patient with ourselves and know that abiding in His word and keeping a close relationship with Him through constant conversation will help us in becoming that fruitful, shade-giving tree.

Just recently I was on another retreat—same place—and sitting beside the creek. "Ahhh," I sighed, "Now am I like that huge tree I saw years ago?"

"Look around, what do you see?" came the familiar Voice to my spirit.

As I looked around, I saw many huge trees, but many of them had hardly any green leaves—only dead branches. "What are you trying to say?" I was worried.

"You see, as you grow big and strong, if you don't allow the pruning, you will look like some of these trees with just a few limbs of life. Lopping off the branches hurts, but it allows new, fruitful growth. Don't be angry or dismayed when the chopping begins—know that it is for good and not for evil! Know that I am the author and finisher of your faith, and I will complete the good work I began in you until the day of Jesus's return or until you come to be with us."

Hebrews 12:1–2 – Therefore seeing we also are compassed about with so great a cloud of witnesses, let us lay aside every weight, and the sin which doth so easily beset us, and let us run with patience the race that is set before us, Looking unto Jesus the author and finisher of our faith; who for the joy that was set before him endured the cross, despising the shame, and is set down at the right hand of the throne of God.

ANSWERING BEFORE WE CALL

Isaiah 65:24 – And it shall come to pass that before they call I will answer; and while they are yet speaking, I will hear.

Hebrews 13:15 – By Him therefore let us offer the sacrifice of praise to God continually, that is the fruit of our lips giving thanks to his name.

James 1:2–4 – My brethren, count it all joy when you fall into divers temptations [trials]. Knowing this, that the trying of your faith works patience. But let patience have her perfect work, that you may be perfect and entire [complete], wanting nothing.

I had been serving the Lord for about a year when I had an accident at work. I was pulling a plastic tie chord around a bundle of wires when the lineman's pliers I was using slipped and slammed into my right eye. I immediately cupped my eye and started praising God. "Oh, Lord, save my eye! I praise you! I know you heal, Lord! I love you!" If anyone saw or heard me, he would have thought I was a lunatic! Yet, Hebrews *tells* us to offer praise to God continually and James *tells* us to count it all joy—I was only doing what God's word instructed.

I glanced into the outside mirror on my truck, and I saw a trickle of blood. I was afraid to remove my hand as I didn't want to see the smashed socket I knew was there.

My boss could tell something was wrong when I called over the radio. He sure didn't want other crew members to know, so he asked if I could call him on a "land line" (house phone) The cable I was working on was in a future subdivision and was't activated so I could not tap into it with my cable phone, but I told him I would try to find someone at home in a near-by house.

Never uncupping my hand from my eye, I knocked on the door of a nearby home and asked if I could use her phone. The woman who answered graciously honored my request and could tell that something was desperately wrong. I explained to her what had happened, and, still holding my eye, I called my boss.

By the time my boss arrived, I was sure my eye was damaged, but I knew God would heal it. I looked at him and timidly asked as I took my hand away, "How does it look?"

He answered, "Just a little swollen and red." It was then I knew I could see because I saw colors from it when I uncovered my eye.

I asked the nurses to contact my husband and pastor when I got to the emergency room at the hospital. Less than ten minutes later, my pastor and some parishioners were by my side praying. Jose and his wife, Maria, had felt something was wrong and had been at the pastor's house to intercede for me before I called! That is Holy Spirit nudging for sure! After they prayed, the excruciating

7

pain left. By the time my husband got there, I was on my way to surgery.

The optical surgeon said I couldn't possibly have seen blood because there was just a little tear in the cornea. I didn't care what he said, I know what I saw, and I *know* Jehovah healed my eye! In fact, I now have 20-20 vision in it, which is better than before!

By contrast, a bug flew into a warehouse clerk's eye and just scraped her cornea. She suffered for months with that injury. I never even had to take one of the prescribed pain pills!

Because I was young in the Lord, I kept asking the Holy Spirit, "Why did this happen? Am I not walking along the right path? Am I not seeing with spiritual eyes? Have I sinned? What am I doing wrong?"

After several days of this barrage of questions, I heard the Still, Small Voice, "You can't help stupidity!" Yep, I was pulling a strap toward me and not away. "Just a little pull, and it will tighten down this bundle of wires," I had said. I hadn't been wearing my safety glasses. What did I expect?

When we let our guard down and do things in a hurry or without thinking, voila! We open the door to Satan and say, "Come on in!" In this case I couldn't even blame Satan! It was just a plain ol' accident due to negligence.

A PROUD LOOK

I was visiting a friend to whom I had been witnessing. She and her uncle were about to be evicted from a trailer they had been renting, and I had come to help my friend pack. Her uncle, "Uncle Jim," was sitting on the couch smoking a roll-your-own cigarette and drinking a cheap brand of beer. His neice had attended church with me and I said he ought to join her some time. "I don't go to church because, most of the time, the preachers don't know what they're talking about," he stated.

I remember thinking, *You don't go to church because you smell like you just walked out of hell.*

"I bet you don't know what God hates," he challenged trying to let me know he was well read in the Bible.

"Of course I do," I retorted. "Isn't that why He wrote the Ten Commandments—then Jesus summed them up with the Golden Rule?"

"Yeah," he said, "but what are the seven abominations to God? 'There are six things that God hates, yea seven are an abomination.' Look up Proverbs 6:16."

I was too curious to wait until I got home to find the reference. (I now carry an electronic Bible on my iPod in my purse —Old and New Testaments, concordance, helps, *and* devotionals —all in one little compact unit not much larger than a make-up compact! Don't be caught without your sword!) "So do you have a Bible handy?" I asked.

He brought out a well-worn, leather-bound bible. I could tell this man had spent *many* hours, days, and years in study.

Proverbs 6:16–23 – These six things does the Lord hate; yea, seven are an abomination unto Him; A proud look, a lying tongue, and hands that shed innocent blood, An heart that devises wicked plans, feet that are swift in running to mischief, a false witness that speaks lies and he that sows discord among brethren. My son, keep thy father's commandment and forsake not the law of your mother; bind them continually upon your heart and tie them about your neck. When you go, [they] shall lead you, when you sleep, it shall keep you; and when you awake, it shall talk with you. For the commandment is a lamp; and the law is light; and reproofs of instruction are the way of life....

I was conversing with Abba (a term used for endearment such as daddy) on the way home. "Okay, okay, I get it. Stop looking down my nose at people who smoke and drink while claiming to be Christians. It is not for me to judge or think I'm better just because I was able to obtain freedom from these blights. I understand why you hate these particular 'sins' and how they

9

pertain to me, but I don't get the 'wicked schemes' or 'plans of the heart'—I don't contemplate who I'm going to rob or murder. How does that part pertain to me, a believer in Jesus Christ?"

The answer came the next day as I was doing dishes and looking out the window. I was contemplating a conversation I had with a fellow believer who made very derogatory remarks concerning my character. "I should have said this," I thought with pleasure. "Oh no, *this* would have really got him back!"

"These are the wicked plans of the heart" came the Still, Small Voice. "If you aren't thinking on things that are true, honest, just, pure, lovely, of good report, if there be any virtue or if it is praise worthy (Philippians 4:8), then you are thinking of 'wicked plans.'"

The heart is desperately wicked. Who can know it? (Jeremiah 17:9–10). Our Father in Heaven knows it and wants to show us—whether it be through circumstances, other believers, or His voice.

A "proud look" is at the top of the list, and we Americans have been taught to be proud all of our lives. "Pull yourself up by your bootstraps. Don't depend on others. Don't trust anyone. *You* are your best friend. God helps those who help themselves" All of these are phrases I have heard all my life.

We live in a most critical and negative society (see the chapter "As a Person Thinks") that teaches us to demean everyone and everything around us—from the president to our siblings—no one is exempt! Jesus wants us to trust Him because He is the Way, the Truth, and Life. His word teaches us to stop planting "weed seed"unkind, spiteful, demeaning, revengeful, hateful thoughts—and use *Philippians 4:8 whatever things are true, whatever things are noble, whatever things are just, whatever things are pure, whatever things are lovely, whatever things are of good report, if there is any virtue and if there is anything praiseworthy meditate on these things* to judge our thoughts! If we trust Jesus, we will follow his teachings!

The Bible is our plumb line for thoughts and actions. *Hebrews 4:12 For the word of God is quick, and powerful, and sharper than any two-edged sword, piercing even to the dividing asunder of soul and spirit, and of the joints and marrow, and a discerner of the thoughts and intents of the heart.*

We must remember that we are not at war with others; prayer and studying God's word are our weapons. It is a spiritual battle, not one of flesh and blood.

2 Corinthians 10:4–5 – For the weapons of our warfare are not carnal, but mighty through God to the pulling down of strong holds; Casting down imaginations, and every high thing that exalts itself against the knowledge of God, and bringing into captivity every thought to the obedience of Christ.

AS A CHILD

Matthew 18:3–4 – And He said, verily I say unto you, except you be converted and become as little children, you shall not enter into the kingdom of heaven. Whosoever therefore shall humble himself as this little child, the same is greatest in the kingdom of heaven.

I had a headache that would not subside. As I reached for the aspirin, I heard, "A child doesn't reach for the medicine when he hurts; he runs to mom or dad." Then I started thinking about Abba and how He desires His little children to consult Him before we take action. So now when I have a headache, I ask, "Abba, what should I do?" Sometimes the answer is, "Drink a glass of water." Other responses might include "Take an aspirin," or "Take ibuprofen," or "Lay off of the sugar." I can rest assured that "Father knows best!"

I remember someone talking about missionaries visiting her home and eating dinner. Every time a plate was passed to them, they paused before they put food on their plates. The host's curiosity led her to ask, "Why do you pause every time food is passed to you?" They replied that they asked Abba if they should eat this and what sized portion they should take! I'm definitely not there yet. Once in a while I remember to ask Father what I should eat and how much, but it is not a habit.

What He wants for us is to walk so close to him that we don't take a step without *knowing* this is where he wants us to go; that we don't say a word without His *assurance*. Jesus spent a lot of time talking to His Father while He walked on the earth. He tells us in John 14:10–11, "Don't you believe that I am in the Father, and the Father in me? The words that I speak unto you, I speak not of myself; but the Father that dwells in me, He does the works. Believe me that I am in the Father and the Father in me; or else believe me for the very works sake."

If I'm thinking "I can do it by myself,"I am also claiming I don't need the Lord's help. Nothing could be further from the truth. I once saw a great message on a church marquee: "If God is your copilot, *move over!*" God wants us to rely solely on Him no matter what situations arise! I can't be the pilot, I must let Him do it!

Proverbs 3:5-8 Trust in the Lord with all your heart, And lean not on your own understanding; In all your ways acknowledge Him, And He shall direct your paths. Do not be wise in your own eyes; Fear the Lord and depart from evil. It will be health to your flesh, And strength to your bones.

Children rely on the guidance of their parents, so our Father in heaven wants us to depend on Him just like a child would his parents.

AS A PERSON THINKS

Proverbs 23:7a – For as he thinks in his heart, so is he. (The letter *a* means I am using the first part of a verse. Likewise, using the letter *b* means only the second half of the verse is pertinent)

I went to an "On the Outside Looking In" seminar sponsored by the phone company in the early eighties. The first day, a black man came up to me and said, "I may be the only *man* who understands what you go through on a daily basis at your job." (I was a cable splicer for U.S. West—now QWEST — in the 70s. In fact, on the second day I reported to work, one of the crew said to me, "Well, it was either hire you or a nigger." I thought I was in the twilight zone for sure!)

Our first task was to take sticky notes and write a short—one to three words—description of what came to mind when we viewed at least fifty or more cards with labels such as: Mexican, Jew, Educated, Masters, Undergraduate, Under twenty years old, Over sixty—you get the picture—placed on the wall around the room. This took us the rest of the morning—there were about thirty or forty people. After lunch we came back and the facilitators instructed us to look around the room.

Ninety percent or better of the comments were negative. Under Mexican, for example, was written *wet-back*, criminal, *stupid, illegal alien, deserter, unreliable,* etc. Every single label had at least twenty negative words.

The facilitators then asked for five volunteers. I raised my hand. They placed a label on my forehead which I couldn't see, but I could see the others—*invisible, joker, leader, militant.* They told us that we were school administrators and were discussing what should be in the sex-education curriculum. We had fifteen minutes to find a solution. We were to treat everyone in the group according to their labels. I stopped inputting any ideas because everything I said was met with raised eyebrows and knowing nods, and nothing I said was valued. Every time the leader or militant spoke, we listened. Anything the joker said, no matter how valid or serious, we laughed. The invisible person was ignored.

After fifteen minutes of treating each other according to our labels, we were told to stand under the card which best fitted our impressions from our group experience and place a sticky note on us that described how we felt. I stood by the card "under twenty" and placed the sticky note (that I had actually written) "wet behind the ears." When asked what my label was, I said "stupid." Sure enough, my label was *stupid.* Ironically, that was also how I felt I was being treated at my job! Every single person (the leader

13

exempted because he had been told what was going on) correctly identified his or her label.

I have shared this experience because I believe we are doing the very same thing in our Christian communities. Not only do we expound the negative to others—especially ourselves—but we collude with each other in treating our brothers and sisters according to our perceptions.

If only we were to ask, "Daddy, how do *you* see that person?" and then treat them accordingly; or ask, "Daddy, what is *your* word for that person?" My, I think people would actually know *us* "by the *love* we have one for another!"

Paul tells us in the New Testament that we can be renewed by renewing our mind. We can change who we *think* we are by reading about who we are according to God!

BLESS THOSE WHO CURSE YOU

Matthew 5:44 – But I say unto you, Love your enemies, bless them that curse you, do good to them that hate you, and pray for them which despitefully use you, and persecute you.

How easy is it to turn the other cheek if I am slapped? Give a drink of cold water to my enemy? If someone asks for my cloak give him my coat as well? In fact, give to all who ask and don't charge interest to a brother? Is this absolute craziness? What happened to an eye for an eye?

Just recently I have been oppressed by a certain administrator. It was so easy to get into the groove of back-biting him with my colleagues. Again the Still, Small Voice reminded me to "Bless those that curse you and pray for those who spitefully use you and quit gossiping!" I started asking Abba to bless him and make him into an awesome, compassionate person who was excellent in dealing with the huge job of overseeing the many facets of the business. The difficult thing was not to collude with

14

my coworkers. When someone was telling the latest juicy story about what an idiot he was, or how he made so-and-so cry, or whatever the latest "discord" was, I had to walk away.

He got spinal meningitis the very next week after I began praying that Abba would nurture him and give him wisdom. Since he has recovered from that illness, he has been a different person. The turnaround has been so amazing that my peers have commented what a change they have seen in him! I am not saying that God gave him spinal meningitis; however, that disease put him flat on his back and maybe gave him time to reflect about managerial skills and how to honor his workforce!

I do believe God allows things in our lives, but nothing can come upon us without the Father's consent. When I read Job's story, I realize how the accuser of the brethren stalks about to condemn, rob, kill, deceive, and discourage us. Even Job's own friends criticized him, and his wife gave him the foolish advice to curse God and die! But God's word also says that what Satan means for evil, God will turn for good.

The story of Joseph is an example of how the enemy of our soul tries to thwart God's purposes for our lives, but he can't. God has a plan and a destiny for each one of us, but we have to be obedient unto death and realize that *all things are working together for our good* because we love Him and are called according to His purpose (Romans 8:28) and because His plans for us are for good and not for evil (Jeremiah 29:11).

BROKEN PIECES

Ephesians 4:21–24 – If indeed you have heard Him and have been taught by Him, as the truth is in Jesus: that you put off, concerning your former conduct, the old man which grows corrupt according to the deceitful lusts, and be renewed in the spirit of your mind, and that you put on the new man which was created according to God, in true righteousness and holiness.

I read a story about "Mama's China Cabinet" with the broken pieces that were compared to broken people, and it reminded me of what a wonderful speaker had said many years ago while ministering at a retreat. She told us about very fine porcelain vases made in France. They are gorgeous to look at just as they are, but then they are thrown down and broken into many pieces! The fragments are gathered up glued together with gold. Each one is unique after that process and exquisite! She explained that is what Abba does with the broken pieces of our heart. That picture has stayed with me all these years! Not only does He heal the hurt and mend the wounds, but he does it with gold tried in the fire!

Shortly after I was saved, one of my coworkers on the cable-splicing crew couldn't wait to tell anyone new in the yard what a despicable, low life I had led. Finally, the Holy Spirit gave me something for him to think about. I wrote him a note that said, "Isn't it wonderful how God can take a tarnished, dented brass teapot thrown away on the trash heap of life and refurbish it? He gently pounds out all the dents, reshapes it, and polishes it so He can see His reflection. Then He uses it—me—in His kingdom for His glory!"

My colleague never mentioned my sinful past again!

Have you been thrown in the garbage pit? Let Him make you into that new creature!

DEEP CALLS TO DEEP

Psalm 42:7 – Deep calls to deep at the sound of Your waterfalls; all Your breakers and Your waves have rolled over me. NAS

The kids at school love to tease new students when they come to my class by saying Mrs. LaVella gets high on HG or HS. Of course, the newcomers are all excited and have to ask what HG (Holy Ghost or Holy Spirit) stands for.
Jesus tells us the following in Matthew:

> Behold, I send you out as sheep in the midst of wolves. Therefore be wise as serpents and harmless as doves. But beware of men, for they will deliver you up to councils and scourge you in their synagogues. You will be brought before governors and kings for My sake, as a testimony to them and to the Gentiles. But when they deliver you up, do not worry about how or what you should speak. For it will be given to you in that hour what you should speak; for it is not you who speak, but the Spirit of your Father who speaks in you. Now brother will deliver up brother to death, and a father his child; and children will rise up against parents and cause them to be put to death. And you will be hated by all for My name's sake. But he who endures to the end will be saved. (10:16–22)

We are admonished not to speak about Jesus, God, faith, or other topics in that vein in the classroom unless it is student initiated. I had a young lady reprimand me one day because I said "Christmas break."

"No, Mrs. LaVella," she vehemently corrected, "It is called 'Winter Break' *not* 'Christmas'!"

I was also informed that Easter is "Spring Break." I call it Resurrection Sunday instead of Easter anyway. Easter is a pagan celebration of fertility, new beginnings such as spring, and worship of the goddess Ishtar. I wonder what people would think of "Resurrection Break?"

17

I prayed many times for the Lord to open the door for me to talk about my Friend and Bridegroom, Jesus; my comforter Holy Spirit and my Daddy. Many times I got to share about the wonderful relationship we can have with Creator God! In fact, I recently had a call from someone who said I had had an impact on her life. She is in a Christian rehabilitation center and has given her life to Christ!

I often thought of the administration finding out about my I anointing the chairs with oil and praying that not one of the students who sat in them would be lost; that seeds would be planted and grow to mustard trees (which I understand are very large) with tons of fruit and shade for all who need rest. Would the principal have fired me if he overheard how I thanked the Lord for His plan, purpose, hope, and future He had for each wonderful life that walked before me in the hallways; that none would be lost but all would come to a saving knowledge of His precious Son and what He had done for mankind?

Oh, if they could but taste and see how wonderful
You are my King and Savior!

DOING OUR BEST

Hebrews 12:1–2 – Wherefore seeing we also are compassed about with so great a cloud of witnesses, let us lay aside every weight, and the sin which doth so easily beset us, and let us run with patience the race that is set before us, Looking unto Jesus the author and finisher of our faith; who for the joy that was set before him endured the cross, despising the shame, and is set down at the right hand of the throne of God.

One time I was at the altar on my knees, bitterly bemoaning the fact that I had been such a terrible mom before I became a believer. I took my daughter to the bars with me. I lived with a man who wasn't my husband for several years. I had many boyfriends. After she went to sleep at night, I would ask my neighbor to keep an eye on things, and I would go to the bars from ten p.m. until closing. Yes, I had only thought of myself and my fun. I was sobbing and remembering in detail every sin I had committed.

After about fifteen minutes of berating myself, that wonderfully encouraging voice came: "Christina, you did the best you could with what you knew to do at the time. Quit beating yourself up!" This also ministered to me in dealing with other people. They are doing the best they can. Until I truly walk in their moccasins, I do not know their stories or the path they have been on.

Our experiences, education, and perception make us who we are. Those of us who believe have inherited the Kingdom of God and need to share what has been so freely given instead of condemning a world who doesn't know the Truth *and hasn't been set free from the bondage of Satanic lies and control.*

DON'T RAIN ON OUR PARADE!

It was my son's tenth birthday, and we had planned a great event. We were going to an animal park that hosted felines. The African park was three hours away, and we were already late getting started. Tony's friend and he were so excited.

About thirty minutes into the trip, my husband noticed that the oil-pressure gauge in my car had dropped to zero! Another hour went by as he borrowed some tools and found another plug to replace the one that fell out. Back on the road again.

We finally arrived about 12:30 p.m., and the park closed at 4:30. Clouds had amassed, and it was sprinkling. People were exiting right and left. Huge rain drops fell as I dejectedly walked back to the car to get an umbrella. I came back and sat in front of the lion's cage. "Oh, Lord," I moaned. "We've had such trouble getting here. Please, Lord, don't let it rain on our parade." I so wanted my son to have a special birthday.

No sooner had I uttered that prayer, when the clouds parted, and the sun shone down. The animals were active due to the storm, so they put on quite a show. Most of the people had gone, so we had the place to ourselves. What a spectacular day!

The rest of the miracle happened when we left the park. The clouds gathered again and poured down rain on our car. We could hardly see through the windshield wipers wildly sweeping away the sheets of water.

Yes, Lord, you even care about a ten-year-old's birthday party in Phoenix, Arizona.

You even care about two people miles from each other needing places to stay because of their work situations! A friend of ours asked if we had any rentals available. He was the bus barn captain and had hired a gal from a nearby town who wanted to work but needed an inexpensive place to stay.

I had just been hired as an English teacher in the town where she lived. We didn't have any rentals, but we did have a fifth wheel hooked up with water and sewer.

I called her, and she began crying. "I was just on my knees asking how the Lord was going to work all this out," she confided. So we traded. I lived in her house and took care of her dogs; she and her five-year-old daughter lived in the fifth wheel. We switched for the weekends. It turns out her name is the same as *my* middle name!

And here's another amazing fact: my daughter was staying with us with her five-year-old daughter. It was wonderful to see the two become bonded friends for years. Whenever she and her mom come to town, they always contact my granddaughter. They often talk on the phone as well!

Matthew 10:29–31 – Are not two sparrows sold for a farthing? and one of them shall not fall on the ground without your Father. But the very hairs of your head are all numbered.

Fear ye not therefore, ye are of more value than many sparrows.
KJV

     Yes, Jesus cares about *every* aspect of our lives—where we live, how we use our time, what we eat, where we go, our jobs, relationships and even our birthday parties. I think of brushing my hair every day and seeing the hairs fall out—or even the hairs that fall out that I don't see—yet, He has them numbered!

     Psalm 139:1-18 - Lord, You have searched me and known me. You know my sitting down and my rising up; You understand my thought afar off. You comprehend my path and my lying down, And are acquainted with all my ways. For there is not a word on my tongue, But behold, O Lord, You know it altogether.

You have hedged me behind and before, And laid Your hand upon me. Such knowledge is too wonderful for me; It is high, I cannot attain it. Where can I go from Your Spirit? Or where can I flee from Your presence? If I ascend into heaven, You are there; If I make my bed in hell, behold, You are there. If I take the wings of the morning, And dwell in the uttermost parts of the sea, Even there Your hand shall lead me, And Your right hand shall hold me. If I say, "Surely the darkness shall fall on me," Even the night shall be light about me; Indeed, the darkness shall not hide from You, But the night shines as the day; The darkness and the light are both alike to You. For You formed my inward parts; You covered me in my mother's womb. I will praise You, for I am fearfully and wonderfully made; Marvelous are Your works, And that my soul knows very well. My frame was not hidden from You, When I was made in secret, And skillfully wrought in the lowest parts of the earth. Your eyes saw my substance, being yet unformed. And in Your book they all were written, The days fashioned for me, When as yet there were none of them. How precious also are Your thoughts to me, O God! How great is the sum of them! If I should count them, they would be more in number than the sand; When I awake, I am still with You.

Can you imagine counting each grain of sand on the sea shores of the world? Yet, David says God's thoughts for us outnumber them!! Yes, such knowledge IS too wonderful for me. I always ask, how can the finite mind understand the infinite?

FEAR NOT

Romans 8:15 – For you did not receive the spirit of bondage again to fear, but you received the Spirit of adoption by whom we cry out, "Abba, Father."

We were on the trip of a lifetime. My husband, my sixteen-year-old son, and I towed our twenty-three-foot cabin cruiser to Orcas Island in the San Juan Islands north of Washington. My husband had the brilliant idea of taking the Inside Passage to Alaska. It is inside (meaning that one isn't out in the open sea, rather on a waterway between Canada and islands). However, there is one point, Cape Caution, that is not protected. The name even gives us a clue!

My husband had been studying books and charts for almost a year; he is an excellent captain. We prepared a lifeboat with emergency supplies, but we were not prepared for Cape Caution. We had been instructed to tie up by two o'clock in the afternoon because of currents, wind, and other unsavory weather that usually happened after noon. Tom decided not to stop because the weather had been so nice, so we headed around the point about three in the afternoon.

Thirteen-foot waves inundated our little boat, and it seemed like eternity, with me hanging on for dear life! I have never felt such sheer panic and utter desolation even in my kayaking days down the Colorado River and rappelling cliffs in the Prescott Dells. We finally got around the wretched point, and I sighed with relief.

The next day, we hit turbulent seas again! This was too much. I was sick with fear and tried thinking about the apostles and some of the storms they encountered. I also tried picturing Jesus calming the storms or walking on water. *Nothing* alleviated the terror!

Then I thought about what I often told my students. "Attitude is ninety percent of the battle." Yeah, right. I could go on being miserable (my son does a great impression of the agonized look of despair I carried on my face), or I could change my attitude. How do I do that? My stomach was tied in knots, and I was sure we were all going to die. "You gotta give me a word. I can't do it, Lord!" I cried out in my spirit from the depths of my soul. Picturing Jesus with me like Peter when he was walking on water and starting to sink then taking His hand wasn't calming my fears! I told the waters and wind to be calm, but to no avail. I needed a word from God! Then came the Voice: "Romans 8:15." I was already hanging on to my Bible, so I readily turned to the suggested passage. "OK, I'll try anything at this point."

Needless to say, we made it back—I'm writing this, after all. We had no major mechanical problems and had a glorious time, I might add! Every time we hit some major water walls, I would simply say, "Abba, help us. Abba, help *me*." No lengthy prayers beseeching the Lord for our safety and guidance, just a simple "Abba, I trust in you." A peace and calm would surround me, and fear would leave!

This verse has been a source of ministry to all who struggle with worry, fear, anxiety, or panic attacks. I have challenged many to read this verse and cry out, "Abba!" They have received the same results—peace that passes all understanding—the peace that only Jesus can give.

2 Timothy 1:7 For God hath not given us the spirit of fear; but of power, and of love, and of a sound mind. The spirit of fear has to leave because we have found out that we are adopted into God's family and are no longer in bondage to the spirit of fear!

FEED MY SHEEP

1 Corinthians 12:27–30 – Now, you are the body of Christ and members in particular. And God has set some in the church, first apostles, secondarily prophets, thirdly teachers, after that miracles, then gifts of healing, helps, governments, diversities of tongues. Are all apostles: are all prophets? Are all teachers: are all workers of miracles? Have all the gifts of healing; do all speak with tongues? Do all interpret?

I was on a long walk in the woods with my two big dogs (a golden lab and a grand pyrenees mix), bemoaning the fact that I had let the Lord down in one of my master's classes at Northern Arizona University. I was sure beating myself up— or allowing the accuser of the brethren to sock it to me. (Sometimes it is difficult to discern whether it is my flesh declaring my faults or Satan's simpering imps whispering in my ear.) We had the assignment of taking a life story and using psychological theory to explain the thought processes of a personal experience. We were given fifteen minutes to present the class with a synopsis of what we found. I had planned to give a testimony of God's miraculous work, but ran out of time before I got to the part about His wonderful intervention. Ending with a bland, generic, politically correct, inoffensive conclusion, I felt just like the disciples who betrayed our Savior when He needed them most.

I wandered in the wilderness crying out to Abba, "How I let You down! What a failure I am! Why did You pick such a loser?" I sure was not what I wanted to be. Then came the Still, Small Voice, "No you're not what *you* want to be, but you are exactly what I want and created you to be. Remember Peter?" Oh, yes, I had compared myself to impetuous, off-the-mark Peter many times. I was a flub-up, sinking in the stormy water, denying the Lord, not willing to be obedient, couldn't even stay awake during the most crucial hour of my Lord....

"What did Jesus say to Peter after His resurrection?"

"He asked Peter, 'Do you love me?' *three* times!" I emphatically declared.

24

"Then what?"

"Well, let's see. Feed my Sheep!"

"And that's exactly what I want *you* to perform—feed My sheep! I have called others to evangelize, apostles to plant churches, pastors to watch over my flocks, and many others to carry out My purposes, but I want you to feed my sheep—lift up, encourage, and teach your fellow brothers and sisters."

Oh, what freedom, to know that we do not have to do it all —just what *He* calls us to do!

That doesn't exempt us from the opportunities to witness to nonbelievers by telling them Jesus, the only begotten Son of God, died to give us eternal life. He rose, thus conquering death and now sits at the right hand of the Father interceding for us. People need to understand they are sinners. Have you ever told a lie? Have you ever taken something that didn't belong to you? Have you murdered? Jesus said that anyone who hated a fellow human being is a murderer! He said that anyone who lusted after a woman had committed fornication in his heart! The good news, or the gospel, is that Jesus Christ paid the penalty for our sins—past, present, and future. All we have to do is believe Romans 10:9–11:

...that if you confess with your mouth the Lord Jesus and believe in your heart that God has raised Him from the dead, you will be saved. For with the heart one believes unto righteousness, and with the mouth confession is made unto salvation. For the Scripture says, "Whoever believes on Him will not be put to shame"

There are also opportunities to reap what others have sown. (Sometimes a person is "ripe"—full of the gospel—and all we have to do is invite them to ask Jesus into their hearts to be Lord of their lives. This is called reaping what others have sown.) If we listen to His Still, Small Voice, if we lean on His wisdom and not our own understanding, He WILL direct our paths!

Psalm 37:23–24 – The Lord directs the steps of the godly. He delights in every detail of their lives. Though they stumble, they will never fall, for the Lord holds them by the hand.

Proverbs 16:9 – We can make our plans, but the Lord determines our steps. (NLT)

FLAT TIRE

Isaiah 30:19b – He will be very gracious unto thee at the voice of your cry; when He shall hear it, He will answer you.

Psalm 91:13b – I will be with him in trouble; I will deliver him and honor him.

We were about halfway between Prescott and Phoenix, Arizona, when the tire on our Subaru blew. I was pregnant with my son, and it was in the heat of the summer—at least ninety-five degrees midmorning. My ten-year-old daughter was with my former husband and me.

I began praising and thanking Yahweh that this was not by mistake and that He had a plan. I regularly read Merlin Carother's works like *Prison to Praise* and knew that God "inhabits the praises of His people." He does not enthrone Himself in our grumblings and complaints! Check out Exodus in the Old Testament of the Bible to see what He thought of the Israelite people continually bewailing leaving Egypt! It was a trip that could have taken twenty days, but they wandered in the desert forty years! (Personally, I want to get out of the wilderness as soon as possible!) My husband was not of the same bent, however, and he was far from a happy man.

Fifteen minutes after we had pulled off the highway, a couple stopped and said that God had told them to stop. Tom had just gotten the tire off and was contemplating thumbing back to Cordes Lakes. We were overjoyed that they stopped because we did not have a spare tire, and we had visions of my husband having to walk about forty miles to the nearest station; leaving my daughter and me to sweat it out in the *dry* heat!

About an hour later he came back with the same couple. Apparently, after they dropped him off at the gas station and continued their journey to Flagstaff, the Lord told them to turn around and give him a ride back to the car!

We were on the road in less than two hours. What a witness for my husband and daughter! What a lesson for me in faith. That couple was not only *listening* to that Still, Small Voice, but were *obedient*!

FORGIVING MOM

Romans 12:19 – Dearly beloved, avenge not yourselves, but rather give place unto wrath: for it is written, Vengeance is mine; I will repay, saith the Lord. KJV

Look at what Cain's revenge did for him! Jesus said if you have even thought of sin in your heart (without repenting) you have actually physically committed it!

1 John 3:14–16 – We know that we have passed from death unto life, because we love the brethren. He that loves not his brother abides in death. Whosoever hates his brother is a murderer: and ye know that no murderer hath eternal life abiding in him. Hereby perceive we the love of God, because he laid down his life for us: and we ought to lay down our lives for the brethren.

I know there is a God, creator, forgiver, wonderful Abba, full of mercy and grace because when I first gave my heart to the Lord and asked Him to govern my actions, my prayer was, "Lord, you know I hate my mother (like we can hide anything from You!), and your word says if I don't forgive her, you won't forgive me."

Matthew 6:14–15 – If you forgive those who sin against you, your heavenly Father will forgive you. But if you refuse to forgive others, your Father will not forgive your sins. NLT

"Please, the next time she calls, let me feel some love in my heart for her. Help me to forgive her." I felt like I was flying after that prayer, and I walked on clouds for several days afterward.

When she called again, I actually felt love growing. Not only that, but Yahweh allowed me to see what life had been like for a mentally challenged mom. No one would even admit there was a problem, let alone get her help.

I didn't realize how Abba had heard that eight-year-old's prayer inviting Him into my heart, how He heard those heaving sobs from the closet after a beating and had put me in a foster home where I received unconditional love until those walls of hatred and destruction were broken through. Now, when I look back, I see His awesome love, protection and provision; how could I possibly hold bitterness and not forgive after I had been given so much? How could I not trust Him and His Word?

A guidance counselor once said to me, "Christina, you have to rewrite the script." (I had sought a psychologist because I didn't want to repeat the pattern of abuse to my daughter like so many parents do when they have been mistreated as children.) I couldn't rewrite the script, no matter how hard I tried, but Jesus rewrote it on the cross! Once I came to know Him, He made me a new creature and is renewing my mind daily!

Romans 12:22 – And do not be conformed to this world, but be transformed by the renewing of your mind, that you may prove what is that good and acceptable and perfect will of God.

2 Corinthians 3:18 – But we all, with unveiled face, beholding as in a mirror the glory of the Lord, are being transformed into the same image from glory to glory, just as by the Spirit of the Lord.

GARBAGE COLLECTING

Philippians 4:18–19 – At the moment I have all I need—and more! I am generously supplied with the gifts you sent me with Epaphroditus. They are a sweet-smelling sacrifice that is acceptable and pleasing to God. And this same God who takes care of me will supply all your needs from his glorious riches, which have been given to us in Christ Jesus. NLT

When I walk, I like to pick up garbage along the way. This day, I had filled a large trash bag in less than the mile or so I was going to walk that day. I placed it by the side of the road thinking I would come back with my van later on and dispose of it.

"Pick up some more trash."

"But I don't have a bag," I protested.

"Pick up some more trash," came the insistent Voice.

"I don't have a bag!" I repeated.

"Pick up some more trash." He wasn't letting up.

"Fine. Whatever!" I was irritated but began picking up some more papers, bottles, and cans. I had debris under my arm pits and in both of my hands. There, hanging on a fence was a plastic garbage bag.

"See, you don't have to have everything you need to get started, you just need to be obedient and know it is I who supplies your need. I will be faithful to give you all the necessities along the way."

Luke 10:2–4 – The harvest truly is great, but the laborers are few; therefore pray the Lord of the harvest to send out laborers into His harvest. Go your way; behold, I send you out as lambs among wolves. Carry neither money bag, knapsack, nor sandals; and greet no one along the road.

I like the adage, "He doesn't call the equipped, He equips the called."

HEBREWS' PROMISE FOR FAITH

Hebrews 12:1–2 – Wherefore seeing we also are compassed about with so great a cloud of witnesses [Paul had been talking about the pillars of faith like Abraham, Noah, and Joseph, among many others]*let us lay aside every weight, and the sin which doth so easily beset us and let us run with patience the race that is set before us, Looking unto Jesus the author and finisher of our faith; who for the joy that was set before Him endured the cross, despising the shame, and is set down at the right hand of the throne of God.*

I had received several reports about my prodigal daughter being on drugs, living with her boyfriend, and other worrisome details. Working as a cable splicer for a phone company, I had it out with Abba during my lunch break. How could He allow such things in my daughter's life? Hadn't I broken off the curses from my own life? Hadn't I proclaimed a crop failure over my weed seed—wicked things I had done in my life? When was I going to see a return of what the locust had eaten? I believed and spoke God's truth for my children—what else could I do?

"Oh, God, please don't let her walk down the path I did. Please keep her from the evil," I wailed. Petitions like these went on for several minutes that seemed like hours.

Finally, I quieted. "Christina, how much do you love Jesus?" inquired the Still, Small Voice.

"Oh, I love Him with my whole heart, soul, and mind. There's nothing I wouldn't do for Him," I readily replied.

"Then would you deny your daughter that same faith?" I didn't understand that at first, but as I pondered it, I began to understand. She would have to walk down the path she chose to find the faith that believers eventually come to. Though my experiences may have had an influence on her, she couldn't enter into the same relationship with God I had. She would have to come to know Jesus Christ, Holy Spirit, and Abba Father by what *They* taught her.

I rest in the fact of the eventual emptiness all tangible objects—job, family, toys, entertainment—bring. As Solomon says in Ecclesiastes, "All things are vanity or foolishness when compared to knowing our creator" (my interpretation).

She will come to the same realization that nothing satisfies our hearts like Jehovah Nissi (God is my banner). And His banner over us is *love*!

KAYAKING

John 14:26 – But the Comforter, which is the Holy Ghost, whom the Father will send in my name, He shall teach you all things, and bring all things to your remembrance, whatsoever I have said to you.

John 16:12–13 – I have many things to tell you, but you cannot bear them now. Howbeit when the Spirit of Truth shall come, He will guide you into all truth; for He shall not speak of Himself, but whatsoever He shall hear, that shall He speak and He will show you things to come.

Kayaking is a favorite pastime of mine, and I live in the most beautiful spot in the world to do it in! I often find a remote canyon with high walls and awesome echoes. I had been having an awesome time in a canyon of Lake Powell, worshiping and praising the Lord. It was time to leave, and a driving wind was blowing me back into the canyon I was trying to paddle out of. I was concerned that my husband would be worried because I had been away so long. The harder I stroked, the more frustrated I became because I wasn't going anywhere. Finally, I put my paddle down, leaned back, stuck my feet on the top of the boat, and gave up.

Suddenly the wind changed direction and came behind me to blow me in the direction I was trying to go!

31

"Isn't this easy?" I heard a familiar voice say, "If you wait on me and quit trying to do things in *your own* strength, I will direct your path."

Ecclesiastes 11:5 – *Just as you cannot understand the path of the wind or the mystery of a tiny baby growing in its mother's womb, so you cannot understand the activity of God, who does all things. NLT*

Psalm 25:4–5, 12 – *Show me the right path, O Lord; point out the road for me to follow. Lead me by your truth and teach me, for you are the God who saves me…Who are those who fear the Lord? He will show them the path they should choose. NLT*

Psalm 119:133 – *Direct my steps by Your word, And let no iniquity have dominion over me*

Proverbs 3:5–6 – *Trust in the Lord with all your heart; do not depend on your own understanding. Seek his will in all you do, and he will show you which path to take. NLT*

Proverbs 3:5-6 was inscribed on the first Bible I received from a long-time friend who had prayed for me many years to come into the Kingdom. It's great advice for any new believer. In fact, this is *all* the advice we need for direction. Praise, trust, and obey, for there's *no other way* to survive this temporary home and pilgrimage!

LEAKING STORAGE SHED

Matthew 6:19–24 – Lay not up for yourselves treasures upon earth, where moth and rust doth corrupt, and where thieves break through and steal: But lay up for yourselves treasures in heaven, where neither moth nor rust doth corrupt, and where thieves do not break through nor steal: For where your treasure is, there will your heart be also. The light of the body is the eye: if therefore thine eye be single, thy whole body shall be full of light. But if thine eye be evil, thy whole body shall be full of darkness. If therefore the light that is in thee be darkness, how great is that darkness! No man can serve two masters: for either he will hate the one, and love the other; or else he will hold to the one, and despise the other. Ye cannot serve God and mammon.

We had been living in a 10' x 50' trailer for two years while we were building our house. My husband had quickly thrown together a storage shed to put our earthly possessions in because we had very little room in our tin shack!

If you can imagine, our bed took up our entire bedroom. Our daughter had the other tiny bedroom. When our son was born, we had no room for him at the inn! My clever husband made a crib between the built-in closets of our room. Above it, he fashioned a few shelves for diapers and clothes—tight fit but, hey, we did what we had to!

Moving day came! We could finally live in our 2,000-square-foot shell. We had one working bathroom and a functional kitchen. Far from finished, it was *home*.

As I began unearthing our precious possessions, to my horror, I discovered mildew had invaded all my lovely clothes, shoes, a Hosier cabinet (brought by my forefathers in a covered wagon from Ohio to South Dakota and finally to me in Arizona—by truck not wagon, thankfully!—and painstakingly totally restored), and many other treasures. The few inches of annual rain we get in this "arid zona" had soaked through the gaps between the boards in this storage shed and had devastated most of the items in it.

My heart sank as I threw away memories and beautiful things. Then came Matthew16:19–24, quoted above. Yep, this is what He means!

It was a difficult lesson, but where is my treasure?

LEAVE YOUR GIFT AT THE ALTAR

Offense comes very easily when I think I have been mistreated or overlooked. I am reminded of a speaker who said to put it in Yahweh's court of justice. He is the only one who can bring retribution and *deserved* punishment. My job is to turn the other cheek (yechhh—did He really say that? Well, I know He *said* it but did He really *mean* it?), walk the extra mile, give my coat as well as my shirt, bless those who curse me, and pray for those who spitefully use me. Am I doing that?

My most recent bout with domineering flesh (what our human nature *naturally* wants to do) was when my prospective renter's check bounced. Of course, it was during the July Fourth holiday, so I tried to be the "good, understanding landlord," even though I had already given him a break by letting him pay less than half the rent I was asking with the balance in two installments over the next week.

Ah, yes, first this excuse, then that excuse why the money couldn't be paid. I was talking to him for the umpteenth time, and our conversation turned into a shouting match with neither of us listening to the other. I hung up.

I refused to answer when he called back and finally listened to his curt message: "This is being recorded; if you take action against me, I've already talked to a lawyer, blah blah blah blah blah." Wait a minute, what's wrong with this picture? He contacted a lawyer? He's the one who didn't honor a contract for a year's lease. Who would be correct in a court of law?

That day, as we were praying in our noontime prayer—an intercessory group that meets at noon Monday, Tuesday, and Wednesday in Page, Arizona—the following verses, written so long ago (ancient and out of touch with reality!), came to mind.

Matthew 5:21–24 – You have heard that our ancestors were told, "You must not murder. If you commit murder, you are subject to judgment." But I say, if you are even angry with someone, you are subject to judgment! If you call someone an idiot, you are in danger of being brought before the court. And if you curse someone, you are in danger of the fires of hell. So if you are presenting a sacrifice at the altar in the Temple and you suddenly remember that someone has something against you, leave your sacrifice there at the altar. Go and be reconciled to that person. Then come and offer your sacrifice to God. NLT

I had been praying for God to create in me a clean heart before I began interceding for others. Needless to say, I vividly recalled my recent shouting match with the renter. I surely hate eating crow, and after sixty-three years, I would think I would have enough self-control so that I wouldn't have to apologize!

When I first heard a teaching on these verses about reconciliation and was convicted, the Lord had me apologize to a person who had been so totally mean and nasty to me, I had retaliated in an equally nasty way. To make a very long and long ago story short: after several days of agonizing about how *she* should be the one to say, "I'm sorry please forgive me," I finally made my way to her locked gate. I was relieved—*maybe she wouldn't be home, and I could leave a note.*

Nope, she answered. *Maybe she'll just say go away,* I hoped. No, the gate opened, and in I went. *How do I do this?* I was shaking.

We chit-chatted and then I *finally* got up enough nerve not only to ask forgiveness for my recent behavior, but for the incident that caused our falling out (which I maintain was *her* fault).

She proceeded to let me know that the car accident my husband and I were in was because "bad things happen to bad people." It just flew over my head, and I never reacted. She also said more unkind things that had I been acting in my own free will, I would have come unglued. Because I was doing what Abba had asked me to do, I know the Holy Spirit kept me from retaliating against her piercing barbs!

When I left there, I was so happy; I felt I was soaring in the heavens for several days. Then came the remembrance of some of the hurtful things she had said, but I was so joyful I had walked in the Spirit, I couldn't even take offense.

I know from past experiences when I go to apologize to this man, I will be blessed.

1 Samuel 15:22–23 – But Samuel replied, "What is more pleasing to the Lord: your burnt offerings and sacrifices or your obedience to his voice? Listen! Obedience is better than sacrifice, and submission is better than offering the fat of rams. Rebellion is as sinful as witchcraft, and stubbornness as bad as worshiping idols. So because you have rejected the command of the Lord, he has rejected you as king." NLT

How he reacts to me or treats me will not be the issue; obedience to God's word is the only thing that matters in our lives.

While I am revising the final draft of this book, I should mention "The Rest of the Story!" Confronting my delinquent renter where he worked, I apologized for my impetuous behavior. He readily forgave me, insisting I had had a right to be irked and asked forgiveness for his behavior!

I left knowing that reconciliation always makes Daddy smile!

There have been times when I have humbled myself to a person who did *not* receive it! Regardless of the outcome, I want to please Him.

Praise Him in *all* things and obey Him!

LET THE DEAD BURY THE DEAD

Matthew 8:21–22 – And another of his disciples said unto him, Lord, suffer me first to go and bury my father. But Jesus said unto him, Follow me; and let the dead bury their dead.

I went to visit a friend dying of cancer in the hospital. It turned out to be the last two hours of her life. She was gasping for breath like a fish out of water. I was horrified at this writhing, gaping creature that didn't even look human.

Another friend was there who had been walking with the Lord much longer than I. Motioning for her to follow me out into the hall, I said, "I thought Christians were to have a peaceful death. It should be a joy entering into His presence! What is going on here?"

The explanation my Southern, redheaded friend gave me helped. When I had to watch my own mother go through various stages of Alzheimer's, I reflected on this simple yet profound truth, and I believe it's a comfort to all who have to face issues with death that aren't the "peaceful, calm, entering into God's presence" that we expect of believers. She said, "I can't find this is scripture, but this is what I think. That's not Maggie, that's her flesh just hanging on to life. God built a strong sense of survival in man. Maggie is with Jesus; her body is just hanging on."

Later, when I looked into my mother's eyes, there was no life; it truly was like her spirit was gone. Some of the things she said were blasphemy, and I knew that she had loved the Lord when she was in her right mind. It really helped knowing that her spirit was with Jesus, and this was just her body hanging on to life.

It had been extremely difficult to put her into a rest home, even though the name of it was Emanuel and her caregivers were Grace and Angelo!—more confirmation from Abba that it was OK to put her in the care of those more experienced in handling such dysfunction. I had always promised her that I would never allow her to go to a home—it was one of her greatest fears. Circumstances, however, made it impossible for my brother and me to care for her.

Being desperate and beseeching Abba for a word to see me through. He gave me Matthew 8:21–22 (quoted at the beginning of this chapter). It didn't make sense at first. As I began to ponder it, I realized what my friend had said went along with this "tough love" word. "Follow me and let the dead bury the dead." Jesus said, (also Luke 9:60) "Let the dead bury the dead, but go and preach the kingdom of God" to a man that said he wanted to follow Jesus but first he had to bury his dad. I know Abba gave me this because He will give me the book, chapter and verse, and I have no idea what I am going to find until I look it up!

I was teaching at a private Christian high school at the time, and I know that I was supposed to keep my job rather than be a full-time caregiver. My husband had also made the statement that he refused to live with her in our house, and I needed to make the choice. She was out of control, and the caregivers in the home we had found for her told us after a month of dealing with her, she needed Paxil (an antidepressant and tranquilizer) or we could take her back!

Paxil! My brother had fits. "It's a spiritual problem!" he yelled.

"Regardless," I retaliated. "She's eighty-four years old, and it hasn't been dealt with. Do *you* want to take her in?"

My brother was in street ministry. My sister lived in Canada and had her own problems. I believe God provided an allegorical place to give us peace about our decision and the verses in Matthew and Luke to let me know that my mom (her spirit) was already safely with him.

I have admonished my own children not to feel guilty if they have to face that decision of institutionalizing me. I do not want to hold them to a promise that may be impossible to keep.

Many people who are dealing with alzheimer parents have been helped by thinking that the spirit is with Jesus and what they are dealing with is the body hanging on to life. I do believe that the scripture about "let the dead bury the dead" helps us to have a good perspective on this dibilitating disease.

I also work with hospice and not *every* dying person leaves this world peacefully!

NON-TEACHABLE SPIRIT

Matthew 11:29–30 – Take my yoke upon you, and learn of me; for I am meek and lowly in heart: and ye shall find rest unto your souls. For my yoke is easy, and my burden is light.

Luke 10:38–42 – Now it happened as they went that He entered a certain village; and a certain woman named Martha welcomed Him into her house. And she had a sister called Mary, who also sat at Jesus' feet and heard His word. But Martha was distracted with much serving, and she approached Him and said, "Lord, do You not care that my sister has left me to serve alone? Therefore tell her to help me." And Jesus answered and said to her, "Martha, Martha, you are worried and troubled about many things. But one thing is needed, and Mary has chosen that good part, which will not be taken away from her."

I had decided to paint the porch just off our master bedroom. It had been painted several years ago, but was in need of a few new coats. My husband was observing my methodology and started making appropriate comments that he thought would be helpful to me in getting the job done.

Finally, I sarcastically said, "If you keep it up, you can just paint it yourself!"

Needless to say, he abruptly vacated the premises and headed toward his shop. Ah, silence. "Isn't this nice," came that familiar Still, Small Voice, "now you are all by yourself. No one to tell you what to do or how to do it."

"Hmm," I mused. "It is kind of lonely. After all, he was trying to be helpful and he *did* make some good points."

"It's like that with me, you see, I have many useful ideas and tips to help you through this pilgrimage on earth. However, you often have your own agenda. Sometimes you have an unteachable spirit."

Ouch! Yes, I am more like Martha than I like to admit.

Yet, if I am to be *like* Jesus, I *must sit* at His feet more often. If I am to live kingdom-earth rather than earth-kingdom, I must take the time to study and ponder His words.

"As a man thinks, so he is," Proverbs wisely instructs its readers.

OUR DARKEST MOMENTS

II Corinthians 12:9–10 – And He said unto me, "My grace is sufficient for thee: for My strength is made perfect in weakness." Most gladly therefore will I rather glory in my infirmities, that the power of Christ may rest upon me. Therefore I take pleasure in infirmities, in reproaches, in necessities in persecutions, in distresses for Christ's sake: for when I am weak, then am I strong.

Our intercessory prayer group in Chino Valley, Arizona, had been praying for six months that one of our members would be healed, but the tumor kept growing until the doctor said that she would die within the month if she did not opt for surgery.

One week before the date she had reluctantly set for the operation, we met as usual at her home. There was a new lady there. She was Hispanic like our hostess. I want to point out that this dear prayer warrior, our hostess, looked like death. I have never seen a walking corpse, but she looked like what I would imagine a zombie to be.

We all got on our knees and began interceding—sometimes in heavenly languages and other times in our native tongues of English and Spanish. I also speak Spanish, and the next thing I knew, our hostess was leading the new lady to Christ. "Wow! I get it, Lord! Even in our darkest moment, we can be useful to furthering Your purpose!" The experience gave a whole new meaning to "My strength is made perfect in weakness" and "Yea

40

though I walk through the valley of the shadow of death, I will fear no evil; for You are with me."

My friend is totally healed with no recurrence of cancer. Yes, she had to undergo the surgeon's knife, but what a testimony to being used for God's purpose and glory in an hour of agony and uncertainty!

No excuses. I used to have that phrase above a picture of a woman with no arms. I had cut the article out of the newspaper and had it tacked on my bulletin board at school. It was a fascinating story of how she had overcome the loss of her limbs when she was five years old. She could drive, prepare meals, take care of her toddler son, and do everything a person with arms could!

On YouTube there are several videos of Nick Vujicic who has no arms *or* legs. He was a Thalidomide baby, and the doctor told his mother to abort him. She didn't, and he is an amazing testimony of fortitude and God's sufficient grace! He travels around the world giving encouragement to youth groups and schools. I recently read that the desire of his heart to be married has happened! He has a beautiful godly wife!

I think of these three incredible heroes (intercessor in Chino, woman with no arms, and Nick) along with Joni Erikson Tada and the many wonderful guests I meet at Special Touch Camp every year when I begin to make excuses for why I can't witness, teach Sunday School, work in the nursery, lead a Bible study, host a woman's meeting, outreach, etc. If he can use a woman on her deathbed to bring someone into the glorious light of Christ, He can use me! "If You can use anyone, You can use me!"

PERFECT LOVE

1 John 4:17 – Herein is our love made perfect that we may have boldness in the day of judgment because as He is so are we in this world. There is no fear in love but perfect love casts out fear because fear has torment. He who fears is not made perfect in love.

One day, I read about a man who was condemning the Bible being in public places because of profanity and lurid, violently graphic descriptions. I've heard Christians complain about the pornography, sodomy, abortion, and violence on the TV screen and in books and magazines. In fact, I have often been one of them! "Oh, God," I pined, "Why can't we go back to the way it was when our forefathers founded this country—when everyone knew you and served you?"

"I would rather have a people who served me out of love than out of fear," came the startling reply. I also thought about our Constitution which states, "A government of the people, by the people, for the people" and how it might be different if it read, "A government of God, by God, for the people."

Recently Page experienced The Torch (24/7 prayer initiated by Deb Fitch and Keith Barnes in 2008 with "Lite the Fire" through Arizona prayer—much like a relay race, a torch is passed from one church to another. Each church takes the torch and commits for a week of nonstop prayer. That church hands the torch to the next group after seven days.) During that time I had also become aware of a book , *The Protocols,* and God revealed that America had been founded on rebellion.

So Samuel said: "Has the Lord as great delight in burnt offerings and sacrifices, As in obeying the voice of the Lord?Behold, to obey is better than sacrifice, And to heed than the fat of rams. For rebellion is as the sin of witchcraft, [a]nd stubbornness is as iniquity and idolatry. Because you have rejected the word of the Lord, He also has rejected you from being king." (1 Samuel 15:22–23)

The realization of our iniquity as a nation smacked me upside the head. "No wonder, Lord, we are undone. We are a people totally deceived," I said in my heart. I am relieved knowing He is our redeemer and WILL have mercy on us IF

> My people who are called by My name will humble themselves, and pray and seek My face, and turn from their wicked ways, then I will hear from heaven, and will forgive their sin and heal their land. Now My eyes will be open and My ears attentive to prayer made in this place. (2 Chronicles 7:14–15)

What does the world see in the Christians of today? Does it see us unconditionally loving each other no matter what sect or denomination? Does it see us blessing those who curse us; doing good to those who spitefully use us; giving our shirt also if someone takes our coat; walking with someone two miles when she only asks us to walk a mile and giving to everyone who asks without expecting anything in return? Do we go out and invite the homeless, maimed, and challenged into our homes for dinner, knowing they will never repay us the favor? Hmm, what does the world see?

We can't change the world, but we can ask God to change our hearts and minds. We can witness one on one to our neighbors, friends, coworkers, and relatives—not by words but by deeds. If the Holy Spirit prompts us to use words, then by all means.

> Let no corrupt communication proceed out of your mouth, but that which is good to the use of edifying that it may minister grace unto the hearers. And grieve not the Holy Spirit of God, whereby you are sealed unto the day of redemption. Let all bitterness, wrath, anger, clamor and evil speaking be put away from you with all malice; and be kind one to another, tender-hearted, forgiving one another even as God for Christ's sake has forgiven you."(Ephesians 4:29–32, KJV)

I like the saying that I may be the only sermon someone ever hears!

POSTAGE STAMP

Matthew 25:22–23 – He also that had received two talents came and said, Lord, thou delivered unto me two talents: behold, I gained two other talents beside them. His lord said unto him, Well done, good and faithful servant; thou hast been faithful over a few things, I will make thee ruler over many things: enter thou into the joy of thy lord. KJV

Many pastors teach this in reference to investments and using our resources wisely. I believe it also means faithfulness in small things.

Years ago, I substitute taught in three different districts. I had lost two of my paychecks along with my checkbook. "OK," I said, "If this is you Satan, *get your hands off of my finances*! And, Lord, if you are trying to get my attention, I'm all ears." The package in the back seat caught my attention.

I had sent away for something to review. Whether I liked it or not the "free items" were mine to keep. I reviewed the product and got my freebies. Then, I carefully reclosed the box so that it looked like it hadn't been opened. Doing this, I would be able to mail it back without paying the postage.

Our postal service rules dictate if a person opens mail, then he must pay postage in order to mail it back. However, if one doesn't *open* the package, one doesn't have to pay!

Busted! I went to the post office and paid the postage. Needless to say, the local newspaper called me several minutes later to say I had left my checkbook there (the paychecks were in my checkbook and were still there when I picked it up later)!

Is Abba concerned about small things? Yes, I believe He is. Many verses in the Old Testament admonish us to be just and true.

Micah 6:6–11 – Wherewith shall I come before the Lord, and bow myself before the high God? Shall I come before him with burnt offerings, with calves of a year old? Will the Lord be pleased with thousands of rams, or with ten thousands of rivers of oil? Shall I give my firstborn for my transgression, the fruit of my body for the sin of my soul? He hath shewed thee, O man, what is good; and what doth the Lord require of thee, but to do justly, and to love mercy, and to walk humbly with thy God? The Lord's voice cries unto the city, and the man of wisdom shall see thy name: hear ye the rod, and who hath appointed it. Are there yet the treasures of wickedness in the house of the wicked, and the scant measure that is abominable? Shall I count them pure with the wicked balances, and with the bag of deceitful weights? (KJV)

Leviticus 19:6 and Amos 8:5 also tell about the importance of not cheating. And if we adhere to the golden rule, what I was doing *is* dishonest and showed that I *didn't* love Abba with my whole soul, body, mind, and spirit or my neigbor (post office) as myself!

Jesus has fulfilled the letter of the law, but if we *love* Him, we will want to please Him!

PROMISES TO OVERCOMERS

The following are my notes from an oratory I gave to Prescott and Page Aglow chapters several years ago. I hope it is an encouragement to you as you continue on your spiritual journey. I had recently been through the greatest spiritual battle of my life. (Several years ago, June 13, 2008, my husband left me for a woman sixteen years younger than I. He married her two years later.) I was very emotional and realized how much my soul likes to command my spirit. I can truly say, He is faithful to keep all that we commit to him and restore peace of mind and happiness of soul! As I reread this and edit it for the second edition, I can attest that He has given me the desires of my heart—all that I prayed for twenty-four of the twenty-six years I was married to a non-believer is fulfilled in the wonderful husband I now have!

45

I began the speech talking about the Spiritual Journal: The importance of writing about our walk with God; the promises he gives us and the prayers that He answers is faith building. Write them down, memorize them, and tell your spiritual foes to get behind you because He has done great things!

I also mentioned the Concordance: If you want to go deeper in the meaning of words, use this. The numbers after each word give the original Hebrew or Greek word, the pronunciation and the meaning—Old Testament/Hebrew; New Testament/Greek. Many times, the Holy Spirit will help you discover the gems hiding in the scriptures. As you study to show yourself approved, He will lead you to deeper meaning and Truth.

Above all else, brethren, I want to encourage you with the following from Spurgeon's daily devotional, June 22:

"As in the building of Solomon's temple,
'there was neither hammer, nor ax, nor any tool of iron, heard in the house,' because all was brought perfectly ready for the exact spot it was to occupy—so is it with the temple which Jesus builds; the making ready is all done on earth. When we reach heaven, there will be no sanctifying us there, no squaring us with affliction, no planing us with suffering. No, we must be made meet here—all *that* Christ will do beforehand; and when He has done it, we shall be ferried by a loving hand across the stream of death, and brought to the heavenly Jerusalem, to abide as eternal pillars in the temple of our Lord.

Beneath His eye and care,
The edifice shall rise,
Majestic, strong, and fair,
And shine above the skies."

Since I spoke this many years ago, I have discovered PC Study Bible and e-Sword, which are computer programs that have the concordance built in. Greek or Hebrew meanings are available just by clicking on the word! We can have access to this from i Pods, i Pads, i Phones, and all the other electronic devices we depend on.

46

I found promises to us, followers of Christ that gave me great hope and satisfaction. What does it mean to overcome, to persevere in the face of tribulation, and to remain faithful to what we know as Truth? As you read the following scriptures, seek the answers from the only Truth there is in this world.

Revelations 12:10-12 Then I heard a loud voice saying in heaven, "Now salvation, and strength, and the kingdom of our God, and the power of His Christ have come, for the accuser of our brethren, who accused them before our God day and night, has been cast down. And they overcame him by the blood of the Lamb and by the word of their testimony, and they did not love their lives to the death.

We are the brethren.

The word *testimony* occurs about thirty-two times in New Testament and forty-four times in the Old Testament. The number 3141 (from the concordance) is after the word. Since Revelation is in the New Testament, we know to go to the Greek section of the concordance. (The Old Testament was written in Hebrew.) We find the Greek word *marturea*, which stems from *martus*; definitions given are *evidence given, record, report, testimony,* and *martyr.* Martyr bears witness with "not loving our lives unto death" from Revelation 12:11.

I thought the word of my testimony meant telling others how I got saved, but the Holy Spirit revealed it also means proclaiming God's word—which became real to me after talking to a friend about my daughter who was taking drugs and living a decadent lifestyle. Every week the saga seemed to worsen. "Woe is me," I would claim to anyone who would listen.

I resumed the Bible study after the phone conversation about my daughter and the Holy Spirit asked, "Why do you give Satan all the credit? What did God give you in His word?"

Ezekiel 37:12–14 – Behold O my people I will open your graves and cause you to come out of your graves and bring you into the land of Israel and shall put my Spirit in you and you shall live and I shall place you in your own land and then shall you know that I the Lord have spoken.

I had been instructed by God when I read this verse to put my daughter's name in place of "your" so that the verses read, *"Behold, Christina, I will open Heather's grave and cause her to come out of her grave and bring her into the land of believers and shall put My Spirit in her and she shall live. I shall place Heather in her own land and then shall you know that I the Lord have spoken."*

It was difficult not to bemoan my situation because I wanted my friend's sympathy, but I started declaring the word of the Lord, and I kept proclaiming it whenever the enemy and circumstances told me differently. The reward came several months later when she repented and turned her life around.

In 1997, God had given me a word from Jeremiah 15:21 for her husband and again told me to put his name in the verse so it reads, *"And I will deliver Corey out of the hand of the wicked and I will redeem [him] out of the hand of the terrible."* I am still praying and believing that word in 2009. (As I rewrite this I still proclaim it in 2012!) What I see with my natural eyes, I don't claim. I hold on to God's Word because He is faithful, and I call forth that which is not as though it is.

When God gives us a passage to hang on to, it is called a *rhema* word. When my faith is being tested, I sit down and say, "I can't go on without a word from you. Please give me something to hang on to." He has never failed to direct me. I'll get something like Romans 8:16 (see the chapter "Fear Not") When I begin speaking it forth, it accomplishes God's purpose.

Sometimes I haven't even asked for a word, as in the case of my daughter, and I'll just be reading along, and the Holy Spirit will say to claim that for Heather.

His word is powerful, God says in Isaiah 55:9–12:

For as the heavens are higher than the earth, so are my ways higher than your ways and my thoughts than your thoughts. For as the rain comes down and the snow from heaven and returns not, but waters the earth and makes it bring forth and bud, that it may give seed to the sower and bread to the eater: so shall my word be that goes forth out of my mouth: It shall not return unto me void but it shall accomplish that which I please and it shall prosper in the thing where I sent it. For you shall go out with joy and be led forth with peace: The mountains and the hills shall break forth before you into singing and all of the trees of the field shall clap their hands.

I can't stress enough how important our testimony is—how important God's words are; we call forth that which is not as though it is and watch it be accomplished. God spoke the world and its creation into existence and wants us to realize how vitally important what comes out of our mouth is.

Then we come to the word *overcame*, in "they overcame him by the blood of the lamb." *Overcomes, overcome* and *overcame* are from the Greek word *nikayo,* meaning "conquer, prevail, and get the victory." It's found in many of the verses where Jesus refers to His overcoming the world.

1 John 5:1–5 refers directly to believers accomplishing God's purpose:

> Everyone who believes that Jesus is the Christ has become a child of God. And everyone who loves the Father loves his children, too. We know we love God's children if we love God and obey his commandments. Loving God means keeping his commandments, and his commandments are not burdensome. For every child of God defeats this evil world, and we achieve this victory through our faith. And who can win this battle against the world? Only those who believe that Jesus is the Son of God. (NLT)

So it's our *faith* that overcomes the world, and we know that faith comes by hearing and hearing by the word of God so speaking His word instead of our own brings God's will to be done. So how important is the word of our testimony? How important is it to know God's word?

Before we leave 1 John, let's go to 2:12–15. I'd like to change the words a little to make it more personal:

> I write to you mothers because you have known Him that is from the beginning. I write unto you young adults because you are strong and the word of God abides in you and you have overcome the wicked one. Love not the world neither

the things that are in the world. If any person loves the world the love of the Father is not in him. For all that is in the world the lust of the flesh, the lust of the eyes and the pride of life is not of the Father but is of the world. And the world passes away with the lust also, but he that does the will of God abides forever.

Those temptations, the lust of the flesh, the lust of the eyes, and the pride of life are what Satan tempted Jesus with in the desert. [see Matthew 4;1-11] No matter what sin you can name, it comes under one of those three categories. So now we know how to overcome, who and what to overcome, let's look at the promises to those who overcome.

Revelation 2:7 – Be able to eat of the tree of life in the midst of the Paradise of God.

I'm not going to elaborate on these words because I would rather the Holy Spirit "guide you into His truth!" When you need encouragement, go to your concordance and check out what the tree of life means—what the Paradise of God means. Meditate on that; go forth with joy and peace!

Revelation 2:10 We will have the crown of life.

Revelation 2:11 Shall not be hurt of the second death.

Jesus says in two of the gospels, Matthew 10:28 and Luke 12:5, "And don't fear them which kill the body, but are not able to kill the soul: but rather fear Him which is able to destroy both soul and body in hell."

What is the second death? It is mentioned in various places.

Revelation 20:14: "And death and hell were cast into the lake of fire."

This is the second death.

Revelation 21:8 – But the fearful and unbelieving and the abominable and murderers and whore mongers and sorcerers and idolaters and all liars shall have their part in the lake which burns with fire and brimstone: which is the second death.

Revelation 20:10 also tells us that the lake of fire and brimstone is a place where the beast and the false prophet are, and they shall be tormented day and night for ever and ever. Jesus talks about an eternity of torment. Who's going to be there? The *fearful and unbelieving (Lord, I believe, please help my unbelief!)* and the abominable and murderers and whore mongers and sorcerers and idolaters and all liars shall have their part in the lake which burns with fire and brimstone—which again is the second death.

Abba promises an eternity with life, joy, no more tears, and being with Him. Those who overcome shall not take part in the second death.

Exciting promises, don't you think?

Again, check some of this out with further meditation and study. These verses will give you strength in the coming days:

Hebrews 12:1–2 – Therefore seeing we also are compassed about with so great a cloud of witnesses, let us lay aside every weight, and the sin which doth so easily beset us, and let us run with patience the race that is set before us, Looking unto Jesus the author and finisher of our faith; who for the joy that was set before him endured the cross, despising the shame, and is set down at the right hand of the throne of God.

Always remember that *Jesus* is the author and finisher of our faith. Nothing we can do alone can increase our faith. Paul also says that the work Jesus began in us, He will complete!

Revelation 2:17 – We shall eat the hidden manna.

Revelation 2:17 – We will each get a white stone with a new name written in it which no one but each one of us knows.

Revelation 2:26 We will have power over the nations and rule with a rod of iron. We will be given the morning star.

Revelation 3:4–5 We shall walk with Him in white for we shall be worthy We shall be clothed in white raiment and our names will not be blotted out of the book of life, but Jesus will confess our names before Father God and His angels.

Revelation 3:9 Jesus will make the synagogues of Satan come worship before our feet and to know that Jesus loves us.

Revelation 3:10 We will be kept from the hour of temptation which shall come upon all the world to try them.

What was Jesus's hour of temptation? Read about it in Matthew 26:36—the Garden of Gethsemane. We will not have to face that! We can only imagine how horrible that hour was. Jesus had to face it—we won't!

Revelation 3:12 We will be made pillars in the temple of our God and we will go out no more. (Imagine, forever in His presence!] *and we will have God's name written upon us. We will have the name of the city of our God which is new Jerusalem which comes down out of heaven from our God written on us. And Jesus will write upon us His new name.*

Let our prayer be in Revelation 3:18: Oh God I want to buy your gold tried in the fire that I may be rich; and white raiment, that I may be clothed and that the shame of my nakedness does not appear; and anoint my eyes with eye salve that I may see. I repent. O Lord I hear your voice and open the door to you. Please come in and sup with me.

Revelation 3:21 – We will be granted to sit with Jesus in His throne even as He overcame and is set down with our Father in His throne.

And one final word:

Revelation 21:1–7 – Now I saw a new heaven and a new earth, for the first heaven and the first earth had passed away. Also there was no more sea. Then I, John, saw the holy city, New Jerusalem, coming down out of heaven from God, prepared as a bride adorned for her husband. And I heard a loud voice from heaven saying, "Behold, the tabernacle of God is with men, and He will dwell with them, and they shall be His people. God Himself will be with them and be their God. And God will wipe away every tear from their eyes; there shall be no more death, nor sorrow, nor crying. There shall be no more pain, for the former things have passed away." Then He who sat on the throne said,"Behold, I make all things new." And He said to me, "Write, for these words are true and faithful." And He said to me,"It is done! I am the Alpha and the Omega, the Beginning and the End. I will give of the fountain of the water of life freely to him who thirsts. He who overcomes shall inherit all things, and I will be his God and he shall be My son. But the cowardly, unbelieving, abominable, murderers, sexually immoral, sorcerers, idolaters, and all liars shall have their part in the lake which burns with fire and brimstone, which is the second death."

God bless you, faithful believers. Stay strong and do not forget the promises to those who overcome while we run the race talked about in Hebrews 12:1!

PROMOTION

Psalm 75:5–7 – Lift not up your horn on high; speak not with a stiff neck. For promotion comes neither from the east, nor from the west, nor from the south. But God is the judge; He puts down one and sets up another.

I work every summer at a camp for mentally and physically challenged people. A few years ago, it was announced that two new people were being trained for team leaders. I was so excited about camp that I wasn't bothered by that announcement until the next day—after I had been pushing a wheelchair with a 185-lb. guest in it up and down hills.

I had left the guest at the cafeteria and run back to the room to get something. Coming back, I was having a grand ole pity party. "It's not fair, Lord. After all, I've been attending this camp for eight years, changing diapers, pushing people in wheelchairs, using a Hoyer Lift (a hydrological device that has a harness/sling and lifts people from their chairs to the bed, shower chair, etc.), lifting heavy guests in and out of bed, showering them, cleaning up messes, etc. These two people came to camp one time—last year— and now they are being trained for team leaders."

The first step I've learned is admitting the hurt. "So You see the hurt, Lord, and I'm expecting You to heal it. I know I struggle with rejection, so I bind the spirit of rejection, and You are the one who promotes, so I leave it in Your court of justice."

By the time I got back to the cafeteria, I had changed my earthly focus on me to the goodness of the Lord and sat down with my lunch.

The lady who led chapel for the mentally challenged group sat down next to me (which she never did before or after!) She talked about the evening service her family was doing Wednesday night. It was to be the scene in heaven when Jesus would be welcoming His family into the Kingdom. All people from all nations would bow before the King.

Revelation 7:9–10 – After these things I looked, and behold, a great multitude which no one could number, of all nations, tribes, peoples, and tongues, standing before the throne and before the Lamb, clothed with white robes, with palm branches in their hands, and crying out with a loud voice, saying, "Salvation belongs to our God who sits on the throne, and to the Lamb!"

"Would you be Mother Mary in the pageant?" she asked. "You will be dressed in royal blue with a lighter blue head shawl. You just walk down the aisle and look lovingly at Jesus, pondering all the promises in your heart that have been fulfilled. Touch His face and then hug Him."

I couldn't suppress the tears when I heard that precious Voice, "So how much earthly recognition and prestige do you want? Do you want My honor or man's promotion? How much more honored can you be than to portray the mother of My son?"

Of course I had to explain what a privilege it was and the story behind my tears, which in turn blessed her. I later questioned what prompted her to ask me. She didn't really know because usually she consulted with her family about the roles and which person would fill them—but I know!

So many times we feel slighted, overlooked, unwanted, or rejected, but if we will put our sorrow and dejection in His court of justice, He *will* make it right! Not only that—He will lavish His unconditional love on us and totally heal our wounds.

One teaching I heard was that when we desire recognition, we are trying to be God; only He deserves the praise and honor! I do *not* want to be God—Satan did, and look what happened to him!

RISE UP MY BELOVED

Song of Solomon 2:10–13, 16–17 – My beloved spake, and said unto me, Rise up, my love, my fair one, and come away. For lo, the winter is past, the rain is over and gone; The flowers appear on the earth; the time of singing of birds is come, and the voice of the turtle is heard in our land; the fig tree puts forth her green figs and the vines with the tender grape give a good smell. Arise my love, my fair one and come away. My beloved is mine, and I am his; he feeds among the lilies. Until the day break, and the shadows flee away, turn, my beloved, and be like a roe or a young hart upon the mountains of Bether.

My daughter had run away again; this time she had left a suicide note. I was attending the orientation at Prescott College for people returning to college. I wanted to obtain a teaching certificate, and one of the elders of the church was with me that day when I came home and found the note. She prayed with me and said she thought my daughter was alive. I also called my pastor and received a word that this was emotional blackmail. As we prayed, he said that he thought she was alive.

Those words of encouragement didn't make the pain any less because we had told this wayward girl that if she ran away again, she would have no home with us. I felt as if everything had been ripped out of my heart and stomped on. The pain and emptiness ravaged my soul. I wept, sobbed, blubbered, and cried for several hours.

Finally, sniffing uncontrollably, I heard that Voice from the depths of my spirit: "Multiply what you are feeling now by millions." What? I couldn't even feel what I was feeling let alone multiply it! The pain was heart wrenching—actually words can't even describe the feelings of anguish! "That's how the Father feels for His children!" the Still, Small Voice continued.

Oh my, the revelation of how much our Father in heaven cares for the lost took away the grief immediately. I thought of the shepherd leaving the ninety-nine to look for the lost sheep and the woman who diligently swept her floor looking for the lost coin. Not only was my daughter precious to Him, but I thought of the billions who had never even heard the good news of a God who loved them so much that He had sacrificed his only Son!

He said, "Read Song of Solomon 2." As I read those words, seemingly for the first time, I knew everything would be all right. This was a turning point in my life. There was a peace only Jesus can give that descended on our home. Visitors often commented on the serenity they felt when they entered the front door. I went on to home school, teach high school Spanish I and II, English, and yearbook in a Christian school, and eventually I taught high school English in a public school.

Jehovah has awarded me with many touched lives! I would suggest to anyone struggling in life, God will give a word of encouragement whenever we ask. James 1:5–6 says, If you need wisdom, ask our generous God, and he will give it to you. He will not rebuke you for asking. But when you ask him, be sure that your faith is in God alone. Do not waver, for a person with divided loyalty is as unsettled as a wave of the sea that is blown and tossed by the wind. (NLT)

He has never let me down, even in the deepest, darkest valleys!

SATAN'S LIES

Luke 10:38–42 – Now it came to pass, as they (Jesus and His disciples) went, that He entered into a certain village: and a certain woman named Martha received Him into her house. And she had a sister called Mary, who also sat at Jesus' feet, and listened to His Words. But Martha was cumbered about much serving (was going in circles), and came to Him and said, "Lord, don't you care that my sister has left me to serve alone? Bid her therefore that she help me." And Jesus replied, "Martha, Martha, you are careful and troubled about many things: [KEY VERSE] But one thing is needful and Mary has chosen that good part—which shall not be taken away from her.

Then came the lie from childhood: "Idle hands are the Devil's workshop."

"Not so," said the Still, Small Voice, "For Martha was *busy,* and Mary was *idle*. What choked out the seed in Jesus's parable about the farmer sowing seed?"

"The tares, the cares of this world choked it out," I answered. When we are so busy doing, we don't have time to *hear* what would make our Daddy smile. What does He want us to do? Guilt is a tool used to keep me subservient to tasks others want me to do or fear of man and what he would say to me not serving in the nursery.

And we say, "Thank you, Holy Spirit, for you remind us of Jesus's words so long ago and bring His truth to our hearts. You reveal the father of lies and give us reality!"

"Who found the better part?" asked the inaudible but heartfelt Voice.

"Jesus said that Mary had, and it can never be taken away from her!"

"And so shall the riches and knowledge of this world be consumed by fire, but that which is true shall remain." Even so, Lord Jesus, *come.*

Luke 4:1, 31a–32, 36–41 – And Jesus being full of the Holy Ghost returned from Jordan and was led by the Spirit into the wilderness. And came down to Capernaum, a city of Galilee, and taught them on the Sabbath days. Now when the sun was setting, all they that had any sick with divers diseases brought them in to Him and He ministered unto them. They were all amazed and spake among themselves, saying, "What a word is this! For with authority and power He commands the unclean spirits, and they come out." The fame of Him went out into every place of the country round about. And he arose out of the synagogue and entered into Simon's house. Simon's mother in law was taken with a great fever; and they besought Him for her. He stood over her and rebuked the fever and it left her. Immediately she arose and served them. When the sun was setting, all those who had any that were sick with various diseases brought them to Him; and He laid His hands on every one of them and healed them. And demons also came out of many, crying out and saying,"You are the Christ, the Son of God!"

[KEY VERSE] Luke 4: 32 They were surprised and impressed — his teaching was so forthright, so confident, so authoritative, not the quibbling and quoting they were used to. (THE MESSAGE)

I have found fifty-five references in the gospels referring to Jesus's healing in the concordance. Notice also these verses:

John 21:25 – And there are also many other things which Jesus did, the which, if they should be written every one, I suppose that even the world itself could not contain the books that should be written. A-MEN,

Acts 10:38 – You know of Jesus of Nazareth, how God anointed Him with the Holy Spirit and with power, and how He went about doing good and healing all who were oppressed by the devil, for God was with Him.

Then came the lie, spoken by many in the church: "Don't be so heavenly minded, you're no earthly good."

"How heavenly minded was Jesus?" asked the Still, Small Voice. "What earthly good did He do?" He healed the sick, gave sight to the blind, caused the deaf to hear, raised the dead (physically *and* spiritually), bound up broken hearts, made the lame to walk, set the captives free, cast out demons, gave us Truth to live by, and upset man's theology. Who could have been more heavenly minded than Jesus? Yet, even I had repeated that untrue phrase more times than I can remember!

We have to continually compare the words we hear in the natural with God's Truth in the Bible.

THE COLOR GREEN

Psalm 34:8–9 – O taste and see that the Lord is good: blessed is the man that trusts in him. O fear the Lord, ye his saints: for there is no want to them that fear him. KJV
1 Cor 2:14-16 But the natural man does not receive the things of the Spirit of God, for they are foolishness to him; nor can he know them, because they are spiritually discerned. 15 But he who is spiritual judges all things, yet he himself is rightly judged by no one. 16 For "who has known the mind of the Lord that he may instruct Him?" But we have the mind of Christ.

I shut the door to my bedroom and locked myself in the closet. "Oh God," I wailed, "Please make Bill stop watching these lurid shows on TV. We have a young, impressionable son. Lord, please, I hate these shows. I hate the degradation and humiliation of women." On and on I groaned. Finally, I was spent.
"How can you teach a blind man who has been blind since birth what the color green is?" came the wise question. "In other words, until Bill knows me, he will not have the desire to keep his eye gates and ear gates closed to evil."

59

Is that to say people don't have consciences before they meet Jesus? I have many of my own experiences telling me I knew right from wrong, but somehow I managed to justify my waywardness. My sins were not important; the priorities were only what I wanted to *do*!

I know God loves him way more than I do, and even though it is so difficult to endure and I am often at my wits' end, He *will* make a way.

Sometimes, I bite my tongue, and often I blurt out my frustration, but I am positive of one thing—Abba *will* touch my husband, and when He does, Bill will no longer be attracted by the lust of the eyes and meaningless treasures on the earth!

TOLTEC ANCIENT TEACHING

I thought this Toltec teaching I heard might be useful for the body of Christ. There are four "commandments." I am certainly not endorsing heathen teaching, but even nonbelievers can grasp universal truths. While the tapes are valuable as far as they go, the teachings do not address the sinful nature of man. Everyone who has raised children knows that we don't teach children to lie—it is inherent in their natures. "Did you get into the cookie jar, son?" "Noooo, mommy, I didn't!"

"I didn't do it" and "I don't know" lived at my house all the time I was raising children. Parents have to teach their children *not* to steal, lie, cheat, to be respectful, responsible, etc.; it doesn't come naturally—it *isn't* inherent. Contrary to modern belief, children are born seemingly innocent, but all too soon their sinful, "Adamic" nature emerges!

The tapes I listened to also stated not forgiving others and holding onto bitterness only bind up the person who can't let go. These constricting feelings don't do anything to alleviate the situation or make the other person feel guilty. There is a saying comparing holding them to *drinking poison and expecting the other person to die.* In fact my own father died at sixty-three of a massive heart attack. His heart was blackened with rage and resentment; he was never able to forgive his sister for taking what he considered to be his inheritance. I am *not* saying all disease comes from holding onto bitterness, resentment, and guilt, but studies have shown that people who are content and without anxiety are healthier than those who are not.

We had a saying at the phone company: "I don't get mad, I get even." Getting even only brings more distress and prolongs the healing process. Jesus forgave us *all* of our unrighteousness. He took the penalty for us. How can we say another person doesn't deserve forgiveness?

Jesus addresses it in the parable of the ungrateful servant (Matthew 18:23–35). The servant's master forgave him a huge debt. The servant left and, instead of being forever grateful, found a fellow servant who owed him a minute debt. He grabbed the poor creature by the neck, demanded payment, and had the man thrown into prison. When the master heard of the treatment, he rescinded his offer to cancel the debt and had him thrown into prison.

I have inserted scriptures which support the following "commandments."

1. *The impeccable word.* In the beginning was the Word, the Word was with God and the Word was God. The narrator actually quotes John 1 in the tape but gives no credit to the Bible. James instructs that the power of life and death are in the tongue. Hebrews says to call forth that which is not as though it is. "Samson killed a thousand Philistines with the jawbone of an ass; every day friendships are killed with the same weapon." Ann Landers.

2. *Don't take things personally.* I need to know who I am in Jesus so when Mr. Accuser, Mrs. Judgmental, Mr. Critical, or Mrs. Never-can-please-me come along, I remember that it is him or her with the words. The words do not define me; my relationship with Jesus, Abba, and the Holy Spirit defines me. The

61

Word (Bible) defines who I am. If someone says I am dumb, I don't take it personally. The person who said it doesn't define me. It is imperative that I know who I am so when these people come around, I *don't take it personally.* I try (key word: *try*) to retaliate with blessing and love. I realize they are doing the best they can and have issues to deal with too!

      3. ***Don't make assumptions.*** Perceiving what a person says is what he actually means without making it absolutely clear only leads to misunderstanding. If someone says, "I don't like you." That's clear, and we don't have to clarify that. (But remember that person also has issues and there are some who won't like Jesus either!) My husband said the other day, "I have to get out and work for a living" in a tone that said, *"Someone* has to get out and make a living because you are just sitting here chatting idly with your friend." I could have assumed that he meant I was lazy, or I could have realized he had just spent several frustrating hours trying to build his handyman website and needed to get away. By questioning him, I might have learned that he had no intention of making me feel like what I was doing was worthless, while what he was doing was valuable. ***Don't make assumptions.*** Then again, maybe he *did* mean it in a derogatory manner—in that case, *don't take it personally.*

      4. ***Always do your best.*** "I can do all things through Christ who strengthens me." (Philippians. 4:13) God is the author and finisher of our faith—Hebrews 2:12, and He who started the good work in us will complete it—Philippians 1:6. "Doing our Best" gives an example of what Jesus thinks of our endeavors. If I can grasp that *every* person is doing the best he or she can with the cards that have been dealt, I can look at abrasive people in a new way. I like the saying that is something like, "Don't criticize a person until you've walked in his shoes for awhile" or I used to cry because I had no shoes, until I met a man with no feet."

      Even though these came from an ancient pagan teaching, we can see God's wisdom in them!

UNEQUALLY YOKED

1 Corinthians 7:13–15 – And the woman which has an husband that believes not, and if he be pleased to dwell with her, let her not leave him. For the unbelieving husband is sanctified by the wife, and the unbelieving wife is sanctified by the husband; else were your children unclean; but now are they holy. But if the unbelieving depart, let him depart, A brother or a sister is not under bondage in such cases; but God hath called us to peace.

When Bill and I met , we didn't want God to be a part of our marriage. We were married by a Justice of the Peace on our property. Two years later, I met the Lord on a mountain, which you can read about in the chapter titled "About the Author."

"Why should I go to church and see some Bantam rooster up on stage telling me how I should live my life when he probably is a worse sinner than I am!" Bill was angry and told me to stop asking him to go to church.

Wow, I sure felt like praising the Lord when I arrived at church—*not!* I looked around at all the couples holding hands or with their arms around each other. *Whoopee, yep, this is just great,* I thought to myself.

Then the Still, Small Voice came. "Remember how Bill felt about golf?" (Whenever we passed the golf course, Bill would say, "Look at that! If that isn't the most stupid sport of all. Can't even call it a sport. Grown men chasing a little white ball all over a green lawn. They have to be insane!" Then he was bitten by the golf bug. Every night until it was dark, he would be hitting the golf balls across our five acres. He even purchased yellow ones so he could see them better at dusk! Every chance he had, he would be at the driving range! And every extra penny saved would go to a round of golf. Yes, he is now an avid golfer.) "That's how he feels about Me. However, when he comes in, you will have to run to keep up. And keep quiet because I will be doing a new thing in the earth, and you will need to follow him."

Maybe ten years into our marriage, I received the above word and I held it dear in my heart for sixteen years.

Several years later, I had begun teaching at a private Christian high school. Oh, how joyful to teach and share my faith every day! I had my cake, and not only could I eat it, but it had frosting, caramel filling, and coconut, too!

One day, I slipped away during lunch and drove to a huge warehouse. Munching on my sandwich behind the building, I had a heart-to-heart talk with Father God. "That's it, I'm packing my bags. I'm not living with an unbelieving husband anymore. It is just too hard. I'm tired of going to church alone without my mate. I'm just going to be a missionary somewhere! Unless You give me a word, I'm leaving!"

Song of Solomon 3:1–5 was the response: By night on my bed I sought him whom my soul loves: I sought him, but I found him not. I will rise now and go about the city in the streets, and in the broad ways I will seek him whom my soul loves; I sought him but I found him not. The watchmen that go about the city found me; to whom I said, "Saw you him whom my soul loves?" It was but a little that I passed from them, but I found him whom my soul loves. I held him and would not let him go until I had brought him into my mother's house and into the chamber of her that conceived me. I charge you, O daughters of Jerusalem, by the roes and by the lines of the field, don't stir up, nor awake my love till he please.

"Don't worry about Bill, he is mine. He is asleep now but I will wake him up when it is time. Keep your hands off and mind your own business. Worry about your own salvation and leave him to Me."

I received that word in 1995 and hung onto it as a bulldog with a juicy bone!

Bill left, June 16, 2008. We had been married twenty-six years. He said he wanted out, and two days after, he left to supposedly live with his brother in California—leaving most of his possessions behind.

I found out he had moved in with a gal sixteen years my junior whom he had met one and a half weeks earlier! I was devastated, extremely wounded, betrayed, and lonely. I immediately reached out to my family of God and received much prayer and comfort. It was still the deepest, darkest valley I had been in. I thought my childhood, nervous breakdown, and then my child on drugs were tough rows to hoe, but this truly was the worst.

One day when bemoaning the fact that I was alone, Jesus spoke to my heart. "What is so different? It's really been just you and Me together these twenty-four years!" I realized Bill hadn't been there for me spiritually *or* emotionally. Mentally and physically we were team players and did our best to keep an unequally yoked marriage together.

My heart lifted and a song entered, "I am free to run. I am free to dance. I am free to live for Jesus. I am free." The time is short, and I believe Abba wants to do a work in Bill quickly. His time for awakening is near.

Maybe a person who enjoys the sanctification of his believing wife has little need for a personal relationship with Jesus. The word tells us that there is no fellowship with light and darkness. I know that Yahweh has a plan, and I trust Him no matter what the outcome. I will hang onto these promises until my last breath is drawn. God is faithful, and He is not a man that He should lie.

So, I waited in excited anticipation to see what He would do. Was there still an empty feeling, a knot in my stomach and a heart that felt wrenched in two? I cannot deny that, but I rejoiced in what I knew would come.

As one pastor said, "When Satan tries to hurt you, hurt him back. *Make him pay!*" I plan to win as many souls for the kingdom as I can and disciple as many believers as will listen to me. When thoughts come in about how unjust Bill has been, how unfaithful, what he deserves, etc., I just say "Bless him, Lord." When I think of the husband-stealing woman and what I'd like to say to her, I just say "Bless her, Lord." That's how I'll make Satan pay!

It occurred to me one day that Satan doesn't want to steal our stuff or even hurt us. His sole purpose is to pain our Daddy's heart. I used to tell my kids, "If you want to give Satan a black eye, follow the wisdom of Jesus. Don't strike out at people."

Ephesians 6:12 – For we wrestle not against flesh and blood, but against principalities, against powers, against the rulers of the darkness of this world, against spiritual wickedness in high places.

If we want to hurt Satan's heart, Charles Spurgeon says in his *Morning and Evening* devotional, September 9,

"His left hand is under my head, and His right hand doth embrace me."--Song of Solomon 2:6

O lift me higher, nearer Thee,

And as I rise more pure and meet,

O let my soul's humility

Make me lie lower at Thy feet;

Less trusting self, the more I prove

The blessed comfort of Thy love."

In other words, the closer we are to Jesus by reading His word and praying, the farther away our fleshly actions will be!

As I am reviewing and editing this in 2012, I want to reiterate I am still holding on to those promises of long ago. However, my husband married the gal two years later.

After almost two years had passed since my husband abandoned me, I had prayed, "Lord, I will wait forever if you are going to save Bill's soul and we can have a ministry together. I'm tired and I am so very lonely. Please give me a sign if I am to keep waiting." Within a week, I received an e-mail that he was getting married July 11, 2010!

My husband Jon, whom I married two years ago, is everything I prayed for and way more. We have so much fun. We fit together so well, too—it is like we have been married forty years. We hold hands and pray together, we discuss the Bible, and he is the pastor of Fillmore Baptist Church in Utah.

When Jesus says He came to give us abundant life, that is not only in heaven, but right here on earth.

1 Corinthians 2:9 – But as it is written: Eye has not seen, nor ear heard, Nor have entered into the heart of man The things which God has prepared for those who love Him.

VAIN CONVERSATION

My biological father hated my mother and was so incensed about a trip I took with her, he purposefully left me out of his will, which read, "I am not unmindful of my only daughter, Christina LaVella, but I purposefully leave her out of my will and do not want her to benefit from my death in any way." He had been convinced that the money I spent on the trip was money he had sent me to pay for some outstanding bills. I didn't discover this until I attended his funeral.

I also found out that he had never forgiven me for a letter I had written stating that he needed to forgive his sister, whom he accused of stealing his inheritance.

He had stayed with my grandmother until he eventually sold the ranch to my cousin. His sisters had received their college educations, and his brother owned another ranch in Montana. According to my father, they had received their inheritances. During the last years of my grandmother's life, one of my aunts took care of her. In the process, she had power of attorney and put all of my grandmother's CDs into her name as beneficiary. My aunt was watching out for grandma and seeing that she was well taken care of, while my dad lived his own life in another city. Her excuse was that she wanted *every* one to receive a "fair" share of her mother's estate.

When my grandmother died, the news came out of what my aunt had done. Dad always expected to be the sole heir of her estate because he had spent his life on the ranch. He was furious and stopped all communication with his family.

Consequently, my stepmother had the same wording in her will and left the estate of over half a million dollars to her only daughter. What was totally amazing is if she had died one week earlier, I would have had the inheritance according to something in South Dakota law that says the natural born heir receives the deceased estate unless there is a will to the contrary. (At least that is the way I understood the lawyer when he contacted me to be the executer of the will) If my step-mother died before two weeks had passed from my father's death, I would have been the natural heir and her will would have been voided.

Abba knew what He was doing, but it didn't alleviate the pain of rejection until I read the following verse. I had been typing a handwritten Bible study that had greatly influenced my life when I studied it. It set me free because I realized that Abba had been my Father all along and had provided for me far better than my biological parents.

1 Peter 1:18–19 – Forasmuch as ye know that ye were not redeemed with corruptible things, as silver and gold, from your vain conversation received by tradition from your fathers; But with the precious blood of Christ, as of a lamb without blemish and without spot.

Other translations give more insight to this passage:

For you know that God paid a ransom to save you from the empty life you inherited from your ancestors. And the ransom he paid was not mere gold or silver. It was the precious blood of Christ, the sinless, spotless Lamb of God. (NLT)

It cost God plenty to get you out of that dead-end, empty-headed life you grew up in. He paid with Christ's sacred blood, you know. He died like an unblemished, sacrificial lamb. (The Message)

WOOD, HAY, STUBBLE

1 Corinthians 3:10–14 – According to the grace of God which is given unto me, as a wise master builder; I have laid the foundation, and another builds thereon. But let every man take heed how he builds thereupon. For other foundation can no man lay than that is laid, which is Jesus Christ. Now if any man build upon this foundation gold, silver, precious stones, wood, hay, stubble; Every man's work shall be made manifest; for the day shall declare it, because it shall be revealed by fire; and the fire shall try every man's work of what sort it is. If any man's work abide which he has built thereupon, he shall receive a reward. If any man's work shall be burned, he shall suffer loss; but he himself shall be saved; yet so as by fire.

We built (virtually out-of-pocket) our beautiful 2,000 square foot home on five acres. Many things had been on hold as I quit a high-paying job to home-school.

One summer, I had determined to finally finish the parquet floor we had in the dining room and hallway to look like the flooring in the kitchen and entrance. We had received a "good deal" on this flooring, and, really, it was so much better than the plywood base we had lived with for years! However, it was obvious that the two floors were "unequally yoked"! The beautifully finished kitchen and entrance floors were shimmering while the other was just plain and dull.

The process of refinishing involved sanding, staining it the same color as the kitchen and entrance, and applying seven coats of polyurethane, each of which had to be sanded before the next coats could be applied.

Many long days of hard work on my knees came and went. At last, I had finished sanding the sixth coat of polyurethane. As I was on my seventh and final coat, with the dining room completed and almost to the end of the hallway, I was sweating profusely. "How much are you sweating for the Kingdom of God? This is wood, hay, and stubble—it will all burn one day," said the Still, Small Voice out of the atmosphere.

Ouch! Yes, the jewels who are souls snatched from the fire of hell are everlasting — they will bring a reward to those who sowed, watered, and reaped (gave the gospel, encouraged, discipled, said the sinner's prayer with others); refinishing the wood floor is not going to matter much in eternity.

John 4:34-38—Jesus said to them, "My food is to do the will of Him who sent Me, and to finish His work. 35 Do you not say, 'There are still four months and then comes the harvest'? Behold, I say to you, lift up your eyes and look at the fields, for they are already white for harvest! 36 And he who reaps receives wages, and gathers fruit for eternal life, that both he who sows and he who reaps may rejoice together. 37 For in this the saying is true:'One sows and another reaps.'

Are we not to take care of our personal abodes and possessions? I don't think that is what the Holy Spirit meant. However, He was asking what are the *priorities* in my life. Am I as concerned about the souls perishing without hope as I am about my earthly treasures?

YAHWEH'S VALENTINE

Matthew 6:8 – ...For your Father knows exactly what you need even before you ask him! NLT

A few days prior to the story I am about to tell, I had been saying that as soon as school was out, I was going to get a pound puppy. Our two big, old loafs had disappeared, and life without a dog, well, is just plain lonesome.

I was driving to Chino Valley from Page, Arizona, and stopped at a little market south of Cameron. I got a double-shot Starbucks and headed out to the car. There was a little mongrel people were shooing away.

It had the face of one of those huskies you see in the Iditarod races of Alaska—some kind of a shepherd mix— and stinky! Whew, it smelled like it had been sleeping out with the sheep on the Rez! (a colloquial term for the Navajo Reservation) "Oh how cute, who does it belong to?" I queried to some passersby.

"It's a stray," an irritated man replied.

"Oh, I've been looking for a puppy," I said excitedly.

"Take it," came the gruff voice.

"A-A-A-R-R-R-E you sure?" I stammered.

"*Take it!*" This time he was forceful. Up in my arms it came; I discovered it was a she. She hung on while I desperately tried for several minutes to get my van door open. She didn't squirm or whine like most pampered pups. Finally, I placed her in the van, and she quickly curled up behind the driver's seat where she stayed for the next two and a half hours until I got to the porch of our unsold house in Chino and showed hubby *our* valentine from the Lord. After the shock of having yet *another* dog—and her staying outside on our bedroom porch all night without whining or pawing to get in—he saw in her what I did: "She's gonna be a gooooood dog!"

The best dog we ever had was Bo, who had just shown up one day, and I knew he was a gift from Daddy. My husband had just lost his dog and was still grieving. He didn't want another dog and believed I dragged Bo home. I had wanted a lab because we went to the lake every chance we got— Bo was a lab/retriever mix. When he arrived, he was very shy, and it took me several days to make friends.

After awhile, he became just as attached to us as we were to him. He would fetch sticks until he couldn't walk. However, most people tired before he did. He would walk up and down the shoreline "fishing" when no one wanted to throw a ball or stick. Bo finally succumbed to old age.

Thank you, Lord! You care about delighting us. Billy Graham once said that if dogs didn't go to heaven, he wanted to go where they did!

YES, YOU CAN TEACH!

Philippians 4:19–20 – And this same God who takes care of me will supply all your needs from his glorious riches, which have been given to us in Christ Jesus. Now all glory to God our Father forever and ever! Amen. **NLT**

I had been asking the Lord if I had been discerning correctly. For several months the desire to teach had been growing in my spirit. I was at an Aglow meeting, and someone handed me an article with bold printing across the top, "YES YOU CAN TEACH!" Abba usually speaks to me in a Still, Small Voice. This time the message was spelled out *loud* and *clear*!

Now came the logistics—how was I going to pay for this? The last time I went to college, it was affordable—times had changed.

The company I worked for had a new plan. It wanted to have employees who were satisfied and in jobs appropriate to their talent. The company appropriated $6,000 for help in any field the employee was interested in. I proposed the education I desired in teaching would help me teach other employees.

The thought of teaching high school never occurred to me. My job, splicing cables, was high paying, very unsatisfying, and extremely boring. It was also very physically demanding. My knees and back were in constant pain. Teaching splicing would afford me the opportunity to keep a high-paid, low-stress job with benefits, yet not have the physical stress of climbing poles, lifting manhole lids, hefting a twenty-eight-foot extension ladder, and bending over splicing wires all day.

The first question asked by the college counselor was which teacher certification I wanted: K–8 or 6–12? (Kindergarten through eighth grade or sixth grade through twelfth grade.) After I sat in on a few first and second grade classes,I opted for secondary certificate (6–12, middle and high school)—*way* too high energy for this forty year old! I still did not plan to teach anything other than splicing.

What a boon! The stipend paid for the first half of my classes, but now the second half was due. On top of that, the solar panels blew off of our roof in a huge windstorm. Arizona doesn't have tornadoes—we call them dust devils. This was a rather large one to say the least.

We found out our insurance covered our loss with $6,000! Not only did the insurance pay for the rest of my classes, but our electric bill decreased by half. I hadn't realized that the panels didn't *store* the energy. I had been doing my laundry, washing, dishes, taking baths, etc. in the evenings, thinking I was using solar energy. After they blew off of the roof and we didn't have them replaced, I realized I should have been using energy during daylight hours not in the evening as I had been doing. My husband also decided to put in a gas hot water heater.

Maybe some would call this a coincidence, but I say it is a God-incidence!

I finished my schooling and decided to actually quit my job with the phone company to teach high school. Had I known that I wouldn't find a full-time job, I probably would still be tied to the umbilical cord of Ma Bell!

However, Abba had other plans—much better than I could have dreamed. I substituted for a year (which I refer to as boot

73

camp!) and was available to my son who wanted to home school the next four years. Since I was certified, I was able to administer the IOWA tests required by the state for all home-schooled children. I also began a group called the Chino Valley Home Schoolers. We were happily involved in wonderful field trips like the biosphere and desert museums in Tucson, San Diego Sea World, a trip out on the ocean to bring up live sea creatures, Scripts Institute, Maracopa Agricultural Center (The Big MAC, where people from all over the world come to find the latest techniques in arid farming), and many more. The students earned their expenses by bake sales and raffles. They learned to keep records of student earnings so when a trip came, everyone had their own *earned* money to go! We had other teachers who had specialties like science, math and art, and we took turns teaching.

I think everyone should home school if at all possible. Who better to teach socialization than the parents? One on one teaching is far better than one on thirty-five! Peer pressure isn't exactly positive any more because too many parents aren't home when their kids arrive from school. Many single parent homes are raising children.

Teachers are the only ones being held accountable in public schools, and too many restrictions are put on them. Students ditch class and are put in In-School Suspension where they don't do anything but sleep, write notes, or draw. The teacher has to get the missed work to them, which never gets returned *and* they miss another day of instruction. We need to revamp education in America instead of putting Band-Aids on gaping wounds!

Then I was blessed to teach for five years at a Christian High School. The last six years of my career were spent in the public schools. I went on to get a master's degree in education, and only He knows what will come next.

And the rest of the story! Seven months after Bill left, I was privileged to be part of Youth with a Mission and go to the Philippines! Two years later, I met my wonderful husband, and now we minister in Utah!

If we will let Him, God has plans for all of us.

Jer 29:11-14 For I know the plans I have for you," says the Lord. "They are plans for good and not for disaster, to give you a future and a hope. In those days when you pray, I will listen. If you look for me wholeheartedly, you will find me. I will be found by you," says the Lord. NLT

Y2K

Matthew 6:25–34 – Therefore I say unto you, Take no thought for your life, what ye shall eat, or what ye shall drink; nor yet for your body, what ye shall put on. Is not the life more than meat, and the body than raiment? Behold the fowls of the air: for they sow not, neither do they reap, nor gather into barns; yet your heavenly Father feeds them. Are ye not much better than they? Which of you by taking thought can add one cubit unto his stature? And why take ye thought for raiment? Consider the lilies of the field, how they grow; they toil not, neither do they spin: And yet I say unto you, That even Solomon in all his glory was not arrayed like one of these. Wherefore, if God so clothe the grass of the field, which today is, and tomorrow is cast into the oven, shall he not much more clothe you, O ye of little faith? Therefore take no thought, saying, What shall we eat? or, What shall we drink? or, Wherewithal shall we be clothed? (For after all these things do the Gentiles seek:) for your heavenly Father knows that ye have need of all these things. But seek ye first the kingdom of God, and his righteousness; and all these things shall be added unto you. Take therefore no thought for the morrow: for the morrow shall take thought for the things of itself. Sufficient unto the day is the evil thereof.

Before the year 2000, rumor had it that there would be a huge meltdown of our computer systems. We would be without food, supplies, water, and electricity. People were buying generators so fast, the local stores couldn't keep up. The "Joseph Ministry," as it was called, flourished.

I was working at a private Christian school, and one of the parents suggested we take the students to his farm to unload a semitruck of wheat! There were underground storage tanks on this remote farm that was a two-hour drive from the school. The students shoveled the vast amounts of grain into these tanks. Parents were irate that the school would take an academic day to do this. That's how crazy the Y2K scare had become.

Sitting at a table during a potluck at my local church, I posed a question to a man who was greedily milking the worried and concerned public. I asked him what he thought of Matthew 6:25–34 and quoted the verses to him. He stuttered something incomprehensible, but what really surprised me was the reaction of the other people at the table. You would have thought I committed the most heinous hate crime of the century! After verbally chastising me, everyone got up and walked away.

Seems to me, we are not much different from the disciples with our doubts and fear. Mark 9:23–24 says, "Jesus said to him, 'If you can believe, all things are possible to him who believes.' Immediately the father of the child cried out and said with tears, 'Lord, I believe; help my unbelief!'"

Jesus, we believe; help our *unbelief*! Jesus asked if He would find faith when He came back. Hm, I wonder…

AUTHOR'S NOTE TO THE READER

Romans 10:8–10 For salvation that comes from trusting Christ—which is what we preach—is already within easy reach of each of us; in fact, it is as near as our own hearts and mouths. For if you tell others with your own mouth that Jesus Christ is your Lord and believe in your own heart that God has raised Him from the dead, you will be saved. For it is by believing in his heart that a man becomes right with God; and with his mouth he tells others of his faith, confirming his salvation. For the Scriptures tell us that no one who believes in Christ will ever be disappointed. (NLT)

I hope that by reading this little book that your faith is increased. *Everyone* can hear Yahweh's voice. Practice being still and listening. It *is* a Still, Small Voice and is not very often audible, as when Samuel thought Eli was calling him.

1 Samuel 3:10 – Now the Lord came and stood and called as at other times, "Samuel! Samuel!" And Samuel answered, "Speak, for Your servant hears."

If you used to hear God's voice but now are uncertain or don't hear it, think back to the last time you *did* hear His voice. Were you obedient to what He told you to do?

If you didn't follow through with what you *knew* He wanted you to do, it could be guilt is keeping your ears stopped. Repent and perform what He said. If you are unable to do the task he originally commanded, say you are sorry and ask His forgiveness. His voice will become clear again.

When you read "Feed My Sheep," you will also understand why it was so important that I put into print the words and teachings Abba has shared with me over the years. I had stories here, there, and everywhere. It was a matter of gathering them all together into one file and then finding a printer. I am very thankful for those at EMI Printworks in Prescott , Arizona, who patiently worked with me on the first endeavor.

Thanks to a fellow author, I have found CreateSpace on the web and its editor has polished this second edition.

I also hope you enjoy reading what has inspired me to keep on keepin' on these ~~twenty-nine~~ years of walking with Jesus!
now Forty one !

About the Author

Christina (LaVella—my name at the first printing of this book) Beckwith has recently married and now has seven grown children, twenty-five grandchildren, and many great grandchildren. I ~~reside in Fillmore, Utah.~~ *full time RV*

I became a believer at the age of thirty-four after a profound spiritual experience. Having suffered a nervous breakdown because of a lack of potassium in my system, I decided after my recovery that I had lived rich and poor, lived overseas, kayaked rivers—including the Colorado River—climbed and rappelled mountains, had been married twice, and had a live in relationship for several years. I asked myself, "If that is all there was to life, what was the point? There had to be more!"

I had been reading several books about medicine men and their rituals to seek truth. I decided to climb Granite Mountain, a large mountain in Prescott, not caring whether I ever came down. I would find the truth.

During a horrendous thunder and lightening storm—the kind that makes the hair on the neck bristle—while sheltering in a tiny cave, I called out in terror, "God if You are out there, help me!"

"I am your God and you will know Me. Come down off of the mountain."

Not really knowing what happened to me, I walked back to my car and sang praises to God I hadn't sung since childhood.

A year later, after a miscarriage, I was pregnant again and desired to know the God I had met on the mountain. That was twenty-nine years ago. I have been reading and studying His Word since then.

I grew immensely as a believer in the first few years. As a cable splicer for the phone company, I listened to the Bible, sermons, and praise music on tape while I worked. My colleagues begged the boss not to be teamed with me because they complained, "She preaches and sings hymns all day!"

Having obtained a bachelor's degree in language arts in 1971, I went back to college in 1990 when I was forty years old to get a teaching certification for secondary education.

My mentor for student teaching was perplexed about trading what he considered a low-stress, high-paid job for a high-stress, low-paid job. "If I can make a difference in one person's life, it will be worth the struggle!" was my reply.

I was impressed with the teaching profession's strong work ethic and concern not only for the education but for the welfare of students. Most of the workforce in America thinks, "How can I do the least amount and get paid the most?" Small wonder that this attitude has rubbed off on young people: "How can I do the least amount and still pass with a D?"

After quitting my job with the phone company, I home schooled my child as well as others for four years and initiated a group called the Chino Valley Home Schoolers. I began teaching in a private Christian school, and after five years I went on to public school.

I attended a master's program in my fifties and graduated with a 4.0 grade point average.

Having turned sixty in the Philippines while I was doing the outreach for discipleship training school with YWAM (Youth With A Mission—some say Youth Without Any Money—was originated by Loren Cunningham and trains people for the mission field), I say, "You're never too old for God to empower and use your talents! There is *no* retirement in His Kingdom!"

Made in the USA
Middletown, DE
29 August 2024

59554300R00046